IN HIS OWN WORDS

GOD'S BIBLIOGRAPHY

Carol Kilpatrick

WESTBOW
PRESS®
A DIVISION OF THOMAS NELSON
& ZONDERVAN

WestBow Press books may be ordered through booksellers or by contacting:

WestBow Press
A Division of Thomas Nelson & Zondervan
1663 Liberty Drive
Bloomington, IN 47403
www.westbowpress.com
844-714-3454

Scripture quotations taken from The Holy Bible, New International Version® NIV® Copyright © 1973 1978 1984 2011 by Biblica, Inc. TM. Used by permission. All rights reserved worldwide.

Scripture taken from the New King James Version® Copyright © 1982 by Thomas Nelson. Used by permission. All rights reserved.

Scripture taken from the King James Version of the Bible.

ISBN: 978-1-6642-3129-0 (sc)
ISBN: 978-1-6642-3128-3 (e)

Print information available on the last page.

WestBow Press rev. date: 07/31/2021

CONTENTS

PREFACE

I believe that God will deliver this book to whom he feels needs it right now at this time, I also believe this will not only be a journey for the reader but for myself as well as I proceed through this process.

The topics in this book are just some of the golden nuggets God has given me to express his truth for those that are seeking it in the Holy Bible, some may accept while other will not, but that's not for me to judge; God has provided the needed truth he wants to convey to the readers, hearers, and doers of His holy word.

Here are just a few descriptions of the topics in this book:

Understanding the word of God and true worship, how one can gain spiritual growth; God's promises made and kept. Getting to know what is true love, being obedient and disobedient towards God, achieving salvation by repenting and seeking redemption through God's grace and mercy which we can gain when we accept Jesus Christ's as our savior.

In times of struggles and trials we can call out to God in his names, he always answers prayers, using the Lord's Prayer and the Jabez's prayer as our examples on how we should pray to God, having knowledge, wisdom, and understanding which are more precious than any metals or gems.

What are Spiritual gifts, the difference between the carnal and spiritual mind, as well as physical and spiritual baptism.

The blessings we can receive from God if we humble ourselves and let God use us as his vessels to spread his word in this world.

There are also self-reflections points to think about for your own personal evaluations.

There are so many more topics that I could not mention all; but are just as important for us in seeking truth and understanding God.

Again, it is not by chance you decided to pick up this book, when you could have chosen another, but God led you to this book, it didn't happen by accident.

God wants everyone to have a relationship with him and not perish for the lack of knowledge, so enjoy the journey with me as we learn what God has for us.

Hosea 4:6, because God's people lacks knowledge we are destroyed, because we deny it, God will deny us from being a servant for him, we neglect our God's law, and he will neglect also our children (descendants).

God is requiring true worship from us, **no more pretending; the games are over,** Jesus is returning soon. The word of God needs to be stored in us so we can be ready to fight with Jesus.

Fighting?

Not in the literal sense, God doesn't need our help but instead standing firm and strong with the Spirit of the Lord within us to defeat the evilness of this world.

We must hold on to faith so the devil or our own thinking; doesn't cause us to become fearful, wimpy, and end up being defeated.

Romans 12:1, when God looks upon us we must show ourselves as living sacrifices that is pleasing to him with our worship which should be true and proper.

As we recognize that our bodies are where the Spirit of God dwells and what we do with it also involves the Spirit of God; we must do things that are pleasing to him so our bodies will not defile his Spirit.

2nd Timothy 1:7, God has given us power and love along with a sound mind that we do not have to fear because fear does not come from God.

Understanding this scripture, we don't have to fear or be afraid of situations or circumstances that will come in our lives because God has given us the power to overcome fear with his words, through faith, patience and answered prayers.

INTRODUCTION

This book is based on the Holy Bible, God's words; it was his spirit that has allowed me to write this book, just as the other writers whom wrote the Holy Bible.

Being obedient to his will leads me to mention disobedient Jonah, who spent 3 days and 3 nights in the belly of a fish, I will be mentioning him later in this book.

I sure didn't want that or anything else to happen to me if I had disobeyed God's will.

And I can't convince you that God has put this book in me but, if you are moved to have a personal spiritual relationship with him then God's purpose for me to write this book would only be a confirmation.

God doesn't need man, man needs God, and he is not hiding himself from us he is waiting for us to come to him, as we are delivered from our circumstances and situations, we will give God all the honors for what he has done, Psalm 50:15.

God longs to have a personal relationship with us so why not start today open up your heart and let him in.

I pray after reading these scriptures from the bible and understanding the contents of this book, it will cause a deep and sincere desire for you to take hold of the Holy Bible and use it as a weapon against the enemy and defeat all that may come against you, in Jesus Name Amen!

UNDERSTANDING THE SCRIPTURES

In understanding the scriptures of the Holy Bible, one would have to know its original origin, The Old Testament was first written in Hebrew and Arabic, the New Testament was written in Greek.

Some words in these languages didn't translate into other languages so the ones whom rewrote the scriptures used words from their own languages to replace the unknown words in Hebrew, Arabic, and Greek.

Scriptures marked NIV are taken from the NEW INTERNATIONAL VERSION (NIV): Scripture taken from THE HOLY BIBLE, NEW INTERNATIONAL VERSION ®. Copyright© 1973, 1978, 1984, 2011 by Biblica, Inc.™. Used by permission of Zondervan

Scriptures marked NKJV are taken from the NEW KING JAMES VERSION (NKJV): Scripture taken from the NEW KING JAMES VERSION®. Copyright© 1982 by Thomas Nelson, Inc. Used by permission. All rights reserved

Scriptures marked KJV are taken from the KING JAMES VERSION (KJV): KING JAMES VERSION, public domain.

Other scriptures that are not quoted directly from the bible, are scripture sited for you, and expressed in a relatable manner.

TRUE WORSHIP

What is true worship?

It is when we give sincere honor, reverence, praise and glory to God, for who God is, for what he has done and what he will do.

Self-reflection: nothing or no one is more worthy; and I mean any and every thing on this earth!!!

Philippians 2:9, we should exalt Jesus because God sat him above all things, given him the highest honor for Jesus' name is above all a name, everyone and everything in heaven and earth will bow their knees giving honor and glory to JESUS.

If you decide that what is on this earth is more important than honoring our father, God and our redeemer Jesus such as; family, friends, possessions, or anything you desire in your heart, then you have made your choice.

Luke 4:8 Jesus said,

> "........It is written: Worship the Lord your God and serve him only." NIV

God will not be second to anyone or anything. God deserves all of you he will not accept half-heartedness.

Joshua 24:15, if you desire not to serve God, then you choose what you will serve and serve it from this day.

Joshua also stated in verse 15, as for him and his family, they will serve the Lord, compared to those whom choose to worship idols gods.

Don't judge someone based on what they choose to desire over God it is a choice that has its own personal spiritual consequences in the end.

Matthew 6:24 Jesus stated,

> "No man can serve two masters; either you will hate the one and love the other or you will be devoted to the one and despise the other. You cannot serve both God and money." NIV

Though money is mentioned here, just putting anything before God, is now your master. Fame, popularity among people, and anything you desire to place above God, you now serve.

Romans 1:25, those who choose lies over God's truth, would whether worship and serve creatures instead of doing these things towards the Creator. God should be blessed for being the Creator forever.

Self-reflection: how can we worship images that God created and not worship or show honor to the creator?

Some people straddle the fence when deciding between God and the world. These people go from left then right and then back to left:

James 1:6-8,

> "But let him ask in faith, with no doubting, for he who doubts is like a wave of the sea driven and tossed by the wind.

For let not that man supposes that he will receive anything from the Lord.

He is a double-minded man unstable in all his ways."
NKJV

People such as these, are not sure of what they want to do, to serve God or not to serve that is their question.

These people are not being hot or cold, God says they are "lukewarm", and he will be spit out of his mouth, as it is stated in Revelations 3:16.

Self-reflection: if you have decided God is going to lead your life, establish a true relationship with him, understanding he has the ability to take care of your needs here on earth, and spend eternity in heaven. Praise God for you have decided not to follow yourself, but if you have decided not follow after God, stick to what decision you have made and OWN IT!

John 4:23-24,

> *"But the hour is coming and now is when the true worshipers will worship the Father in Spirit and truth; for the Father is seeking such to worship Him.*
>
> *God is spirit, and those who worship Him must worship in Spirit and truth."* NKJV

SPIRITUAL GROWTH

God is refining us for his purpose, the work he does will benefit us because we will see in ourselves and with our attitude towards others.

Having spiritual growth will allow us to step out of our comfort zone and minister to others about God. But first we must go through trials and temptations as God increases his abilities in us.

Self-reflection: God is not going to allow us to go among the wolves and not be equipped to minister about his word. He is not going to make us a captain of a luxury cruise ship if we have never steered a boat.

Jesus prepared the twelve disciples before sending them off two by two ministering to the people about repentance.

God can use true believers to benefit non-believers as they watch and observe these believers; it might compel non-believers to come to God.

As we talk about our walk with God with others they may began to notice how we go through difficult times, they might be thinking and wondering if what we say and do; when it comes to trusting and believing in God is all talk, or do we truly have faith in him.

God is able to provide us with the strength we need to endure struggles and he will receive all the glory. If our walk is sincere, those that see for themselves that trusting and believing in God is indeed worth it, might also start to begin to have a personal spiritual relationship with him.

We need God in our daily lives (every second, of every minute, of every hour), he is waiting for us to pray to him so he can lead us in the right way in which he wants us to go; now it won't always be good and we must endure some type of suffering.

People of God, already know there will be struggles as long as we are on this earth, but we also know it is temporary and God will continue to strengthen us as we go through.

As we endure the hardships, it will increase our faith in God and after leaving this earth we will receive eternal life. There we will rejoice in overcoming the troubles of this world and celebrate with everyone else, who has also overcame.

2nd Timothy 2:3

> "You therefore must endure hardship as a good solider of Jesus Christ." NKJV

Revelation 21:7, whoever believes in God will receive all his inheritance because we are now his sons and daughters, and he is our God.

People who are not quite sure about God will see our walk in faith, their curiosity may be peaked, we could be the example that could lead them to God and not even know it. So we must be mindful of what we say and do, for we are the light of the world that helps guide people to God.

Matthew 5:14, we are the light of the world, a city on the hill that cannot be hidden.

When we encounter a non-believer and give our testimony about God, we are planting a seed; when someone else gives their testimony to the non-believer, they are watering that seed and God will give the increase by touching that person's heart if they are willing to receive his truth.

1st Corinthians 3:6, one plants, another waters, but God gives the increase.

The people, who blame God for all the bad situations or circumstances in their lives, don't seem to realize it may be their own choice to be in that state, God doesn't force himself upon any one.

Matthew 23:37, Jesus mourned over Jerusalem, he would have loved to have taken the children of Jerusalem into him, the same way a mother hen gathers in her chicks under her wings but because the children of Jerusalem refuse to let him and he did not force himself on them.

Self-reflection: but isn't it so ironic when things in people's lives are going so well nothing about God is acknowledged but soon as a bump in the road it is all God's fault.

That is so not true, we have free will to make choices and decisions; however, without seeking the guidance from God we want to blame him for allowing us to go through some rough patches, without seeking his guidance, we are all capable of messing up our own lives.

After the Children of Israel, saw all the wonders that God had performed to free them from the hand of Pharaoh, they still were not willing to wait for his guidance.

The Israelites, became impatient waiting for Moses to return from the mountain; were he was speaking to God. The people went to Aaron to request an idol image to be made for them to worship,

Aaron was hesitate at first but gave in. He ordered the people to collect gold from their possessions to create a golden image for them to worship. (Exodus 32:1-4)

God spoke to Moses letting him know that the Children of Israel have corrupted themselves by creating an idol image, God called the Israelites "*stiff-necked*" (meaning hard-headedness) and wanted to punish them because of their wickedness, when Moses returned from the mountain, he saw the Israelites worshiping and dancing before the golden image he became mad and destroyed the image in the fire that was in front of it. Moses asked Aaron, what did the people do to him; to cause him to create an image that was a sin against God, (Exodus 32:19-21).

Moses went back up to the mountain to speak to God and sought to seek repentance on behalf of the Children of Israel's sin. God told Moses to lead the people to place he had prepared for them and he would punish them for the sin they committed against him. God plagued the people because of the image that they had Aaron create, (Exodus 32:30-35).

Because the Israelites were not patient enough to wait for Moses' return and receive the guidance and leadership from God, they took matters in their own hands and decided to create an image they could worship, which was a sin, they didn't consider the cost of their action, which caused a plague among the people.

False prophets are known for attracting people who they think are spiritually weak. Their teachings are mistaken thoughts and ideas based on the words of God to condemn or to control others minds based on their "spiritual" logics.

1st John 4:1, love one's, do not be tricked by every spirit but test it to see if it comes from God, because there are false prophets in this world.

Be mindful of those that have come to deceive us it's not just Satan but false prophets whom say they have come in God's name.

In relationships, God wants us to be compatible with our mates and if we choose to mate with someone not compatible to us, we may not be well prepared to handle circumstances that occur in relationships or marriages such as friends, family, finance, children, and physical life changes; God's purposes for our lives work out according to his will.

2nd Corinthians 6:14, don't be bounded with an unbeliever how can good be with evil, or the light having companionship with the dark.

Self-reflection: As we increase our spiritual growth, no matter what occurs in our lives, God will be there to lead us to the destination he has for us.

Matthew 17:20, if we have the faith of a small seed we can do the impossible with God by our side.

The "mustard seed" of faith, means that your faith doesn't have to be large or enormous but even the smallest amount of faith can cause the impossible to be possible.

Self-reflection: Building a strong and sincere relationship with God will ensure spiritual growth for the desires you have requested from him.

Matthew 7:7-8, Jesus stated

> *"Ask and it will be given to you, seek and you will find, knock and it will be opened to you.*
>
> *For everyone who asks receives, he who seeks finds, and to him who knocks it will be opened." NKJV*

God will not bless you for something or someone you don't need that may be harmful to you not just physically and mentally, but spiritually.

God will get you to your purpose, again, you will have to first go through the suffering and sacrifices to get to the blessings.

Romans 8:17, if we are children of God we will receive the inheritance as co-heirs with Jesus as we share in his suffering we shall also share in his glory.

If God gave us the desires of our heart and we are not prepared to handle it, God failed us.

But that's a LIE!!!! **God cannot fail** it's not in him to do so, because he is God, *"I am that I am"*, Exodus 3:14 KJV.

Joshua 21:45, not one of God's good promises have failed, all was fulfilled to Israel.

Once God has led us to our purpose we should praise, give honor and glory to him for what he has done.

How to understand God's will is by reading his word, which can prepare us for what he knows will be best thing for our lives, his blessings are like opening a door no man can close, closing doors no man can open, Isaiah 22:22.

How good is God?

So good that after we have been broken, molded, refined, and polished he rewards us for enduring through it all.

We are now new creatures through Christ Jesus no longer bound by sin for we have been washed in the blood that Jesus shed on the cross.

Matthew 26:28, Jesus said,

> "For this is My blood of the new covenant which is shed
> for many for the remission of sins." NKJV

2nd Corinthians 5:17, if we are in Christ our old ways are now passed away and we have become new creatures all things have become new.

We now are new people in the way we interact with others and that we are no longer bound to our sinful ways.

Building a relationship with God allows for his guidance and leadership to be a daily practice of reading the bible, prayer and meditating on the scriptures.

God created you, me, everything upon heaven and earth there was no big bang or Darwin theory, sorry not sorry, to the scientists, not everything can be explained with only what you can feel, see, smell, taste, and touch type of logic.

Genesis 1:1

> "In the beginning God created the heavens and the
> earth" NIV.

Gaining spiritual growth, strong and true, is by trusting and believing in God it's a practice style we must work on a daily basis in continuing our relationship with him.

Self-reflection: some people work out their bodies to strengthen areas that are weak or they want to tone up, just think if we strengthen ourselves in God through prayer, faith, believing, and having sincere repentance what we would our spiritual bodies (in a sense) look like?

MEN AND WOMEN CHOSEN BY GOD

The bible consists of men whom were just like us and God used them for his glory to show that he can use anyone at any time in their lives. Here are some of these men:

Abraham lied about his wife being his sister so the Egyptians would take her and for him not be killed, Genesis 20:2.

Jacob traded the food he had cooked for the birthright of his older brother, Esau, because he saw Esau was starving for substance, Genesis 25:29-33. Jacob also cheated Esau out of his blessing by impersonating Esau to their blind father, Isaac, whom was on his deathbed, Genesis 27:10-29.

King David took his soldiers wife, Bathsheba, as Uriah was fighting for him. Bathsheba was bathing and David noticed her, and then told his messengers to bring Bathsheba to him and he had relations with her, 2nd Samuel 11:2-4.

Matthew was a tax collector at that time they were considered sinners. Jesus requested to meet with Matthew in his home to speak with him; the Pharisees saw it and couldn't understand why Jesus was conversing with sinners, Matthew 9:9-11.

Peter told Jesus he was a sinful man; Luke 5:8.

Saul (Paul), on his way to Damascus to arrest Christians, encountered Jesus. He asked Saul *"why are you persecuting me."*, and Jesus caused Saul to go blind, Acts 9:1-16.

After God used these men for his purpose he blessed them:

God told Abraham he would become the father of many nations, Genesis 17:4-5.

Jacob became the father of a son who became the right hand man to Pharaoh of Egypt saving Jacob, his family and the other Israelites when the famine struck their land, Genesis 41: 37-44, 42:5-6, and 46:4-7.

David was considered a man after God's own heart, 1st Samuel 13:14.

2nd Samuel 12:16-24 King David pleaded with God in the temple to spare their first child by not eating or drinking, and laying all night on the ground in a sackcloth. On the seventh day the child died, when David found out that the child had died he got up and cleaned himself up eat and drink then went to comfort Bathsheba. Their second child became the wisest person ever on earth, Solomon.

After Jesus spoke to Matthew, he became one of Jesus' disciples, Matthew 9: 10-12.

Peter became a disciple of Jesus after trusting in him and not just by seeing the miracle he performed but the words he spoke pierced Peter's heart, making him a fisherman among men, Luke 5:10-11.

After Saul, (Paul), encounter with Jesus on the road to Damascus, he was converted, baptized, and became an apostle of Jesus Christ, Acts 9:17-18.

As women, we go through some of the same things as men; however, we are also are seen differently in some aspects of how we look, act, dress and even being a b**** for having a strong mind.

In the bible, Jesus spoke to women whom society considered less desirable or least respected during his time on earth; though it is still present today.

These women after speaking and listening to Jesus became believers:

The woman who washed Jesus feet with her tears and dried them with her hair, Luke 7:36-46.

After washing and drying Jesus' feet, the woman was blessed by Jesus, (47-50).

The woman at the well having many husbands and the one she had at that time was not her own, John 4:7-18.

Jesus requested some water from the woman at the well and began telling her, the woman's life story, his words pierced the woman's heart and she gave her testimony to the town's people about Jesus. When he got into town they listened to Jesus speak and many Samaritans became believers, John 4: 21-4.

The woman sentenced to be stoned for getting caught in adultery, John 8:1-6.

Jesus made a remark to the mob crowd, *"He without sin throws the first stone"* and no one was able to throw a single rock. Jesus questioned the woman, *"Where are your accusers?"* She found none, Jesus then stated that he didn't condemn her either and said *"go and sin no more"*, (7-11) NKJV.

She became a follower of Jesus, John 19:25 and 20:1-8.

This woman caught in Adultery is considered to be Mary Magdalene by some scholars; she was one of the women at Jesus' crucifixion and also among the women Jesus met after his resurrection, Matthew 28:1-10 and John 20:15-18.

Now, you can see these men and women were by no means perfect, but they allowed God to use them for his purpose. Jesus didn't judge any one of them and I believe in my spirit, they rejoiced in the love he had shown them.

Jesus' love for them exceeded their sins, isn't that wonderful to know JESUS LOVES US!!!!!

Receiving the word of God and salvation, as they went through situations and circumstances, these men and women trusted in the Father and Son that they would see them through it all.

Self-reflection: How do you want God to use you? He will show your purpose just trust in Him.

TRUE LOVE

When the Passion of Christ movie came out many, many years ago a song writer made a Christian music video using clips of the movie.

I was in awe of that video, actually seeing the whips, beatings, and the torture Jesus endured, with the song in the background made me cry not from the pain he suffered, oh Jesus suffered, but by the love he showed while enduring it all.

The love God has for us is the reason Jesus took our place and died. He could have let us fall and perish for we are a sinful people, but he did it out of LOVE!!!!

Why is love so hard to give or receive these days? Everyone seems to be out for themselves whether for power, wealth, fame or fortune. People climbing on top of one another to get ahead and everyone on the bottom suffer more.

People don't love unless it is family or friends; even then, there may not be love.

Jesus showed us TRUE LOVE not only by dying for us; but also showed LOVE before his death.

He raised a child and a man from death, Matthew 9:23-25 and John 11: 1-16.

A crippled man walked, Mark 2:2-12

Two blind men were able to see, Matthew 9:27-30.

Healed a woman with a condition of blood, Matthew 9:20-22

And so many others Jesus helped while he was on this earth without needing any recognition; he even told the two men he gave sight *"see that no man know it"* but they told anyway, Matthew 9:30-3, KJV.

Self-reflection: would you want the opportunity to be acknowledged by the world for your actions and deeds only to receive superficial praises, honor, and accolades or be recognized by God when you do actions and deeds secretly then be rewarded greatly.

Matthew 6:4, what charitable actions we perform in secret God our father will bless us openly for the world to see.

You don't have to boast about what you have done for others but doing it with a sincere heart without even considering the blessings God gives, but simply showing LOVE!!!!

As I was continuing to write this book, the Coronavirus is now a Global Pandemic, and everyone is supposed to be in their homes. No social gatherings, no work or school, not even gathering at the house of prayer.

No vacation abroad, state to state travel, many states have completely locked down; 4 states, including Arkansas, choose not to shut down as of April 3, 2020.

Everyone on television is trying to get the word out about what needs to be done to get the virus past us and move forward.

But we know God is in control of this and when he is ready for this to pass it will. I personally think, God is saying that since we have taken him (God) out of everything on this earth, he will be acknowledged and honored on earth and this is a punishment to us for not obeying the one who created us; we have decided to go our own way and not recognize GOD.

Lamentations 3:37-42

> "Who is he who speaks and it comes to pass, when the Lord has not command it?
>
> Is it not from the mouth of the Most High that woe and well-being proceed?
>
> Why should a living man complain, a man for the punishment of his sins?
>
> Let us search out and examine our ways, and turn back to the Lord.
>
> Let us lift our hearts and hands to God in heaven.
>
> We have transgressed and rebelled: you have not pardoned" NKJV

God is not pleased with the world (people); they have turned away from him and decided to become their own god.

Self-reflection: Who is ruler over your life? Is it you, then you are your own god and this is not what God wants us to be, we need to acknowledge we are his children and he is Our Father.

Jeremiah 32:38-40

"They shall be My people and I will be their God.

Then I will give them one heart and one way, that they may fear Me forever, for the good of them and their children after them.

And I will make an everlasting covenant with them that I will not turn away from doing them good; but I will put My fear in their hearts so that they will not depart from Me." NKJV

Romans 10:3, for those being foolish towards God's righteousness, establishing their own righteousness, have not yielded to the righteousness of God.

We need God in all we do or he will show us our error which is why we are now seeing more people on television praying and asking God to aid in this pandemic.

God will provide the cure that man will use to combat the virus but will man recognize this or will man take credit for providing the world with a cure and ignore the work of God.

Matthew 24:6-8, Jesus mentions wars and rumor of wars, famine, plaques and diseases upon the earth. Nations will fight against other nations. Though these things must come to pass do not be concerned for the end is not yet, for these will become times of sorrow.

Luke 21:11

Jesus says these same words:

"There will be great earthquakes, famines and pestilences in various places, and fearful events and great signs from heaven." NIV

1st John 4:16, we all know and believe God has love for us all because he is love; we endure in him as God endures in us.

God's words are manifesting and are being fulfilled. It is time to get right with Him or not, it is YOUR CHOICE!!! Heaven and Hell are true, so let's go deeper into that statement.

HEAVENS AND HELL

There are three levels of heaven, to confirm this from scripture, Genesis 1:1 reads *"In the beginning God created the heavens and the earth."* As we can see the word heaven has an "s" at the end, so as in primary school we were taught "s" at the end of a word means more than one.

The first heaven is the ozone that surrounds the atmosphere of this world, Genesis 1:20.

The second heaven, represents the expansion of the universe (sun, moon, stars, planets, and comets), Genesis 1:17.

It has been said that when God took Enoch and he went to heaven, Genesis 5:24.

This theory has also been said about Moses, when he died, God took him where no one would ever find his body, Deuteronomy 34:5-6.

Elijah, who was taken in a chariot of fire, (appearing with horses of fire), up in a whirlwind, 2nd Kings 2:11.

John 3:13 Jesus said:

> *"No one has ascended to heaven but He who came from heaven that is the Son of Man, who is in heaven"* NKJV

We all know who Jesus was referring to, HIMSELF.

The statement Jesus Christ made confirms that, Enoch, Moses and Elijah did not go to Heaven but to a heaven which one, we do not know; only God knows.

This is the vision the apostle John received from the Holy Spirit while on the Island of Patmos (Revelation 1:9):

The third HEAVEN is made of gold and other precious metals, the precious stones such as rubies, sapphires, garnets, emeralds, and others, just imagine more precious stones than the ones we already know. Crystal floors smooth as glass all the colors of the rainbow maybe even more, Revelation 4: 3, 6.

This Kingdom of Heaven is where God, Jesus, Holy Spirit, 4 Beasts with many eyes, and 420 elders reside, (4).

God is sitting on the throne and the seven Spirits of God represented by seven fire burning lamps that are before the throne, (5).

John gave a description of each beast in verses 7 and 8.

John wrote that these beasts in Heaven were singing and praising God saying *"Holy, Holy, Holy, and Lord God Almighty."* The beasts acknowledged God by giving him glory, honor, and thanks as he sat on the throne. The elders fell down and casted their crowns to God saying *"thou art worthy, O Lord, to receive glory and honor and power......"* (8-10) KJV

Revelation chapter 5, John describes how Jesus whom died and redeemed us back to God, was the only one able to receive the sealed book that was held by God and all that were in Heaven worshipped

Jesus for who he was, the redeemer, lamb of God whom was slain, and the Lion of David, (5-14).

Self-reflection: think about being in the presence of God and Jesus' glory forever shining, your immortal spirit in a white rob and a crown on your head.

Revelation 6: 9, 10 and11

> *"When he opened the fifth seal I saw under the altar the souls of those who had been slain for the word of God and for testimony which they held.*
>
> *And they cried with a loud voice, saying, how long, O Lord, holy and true until You judge and avenge our blood on those who dwell on the earth?*
>
> *Then a white rob was given to each of them and it was said to them that they should rest a little while longer until both the number of their fellow servants and their brethren, who would be killed as they were was completed."* NKJV

2nd Timothy 4:8, at the end, we will receive a crown of righteousness, from Jesus who is the judge of righteousness, will give to us who all have loved his presence.

1st Corinthians 15:53-54

> *"For this corruptible must put on incorruption, and this mortal must put on immortality.*
>
> *So when this corruptible has put on incorruption, and this mortal has put on immortality, then shall be brought*

to pass the say that it is written: Death is swallowed up in victory." NKJV

Not this body we have now but a perfect immortal spirit free from; sickness, aches, pains, aging, and death will be no more, Revelation 21:4.

We will be able to talk to God, Jesus, and everyone, all on one accord, peace, love and harmony all in an eternal occurrence, time is non-existence.

No more sleeping because there no need to be tired and no more eating there will no need, just being in the presence of God and Jesus will be the fulfillment.

Hell is a much different place; it is where the Dragon aka Satan aka Devil, aka Belial, his angels (demons); and those whose name is not written in God's Book of Life will reside! Revelation 13:8 and 20:13-15.

There was a great war in heaven, Satan and his angels fought against God and his angels, Satan was casted out of heaven to earth along with his demons, Luke 10:18 and Revelation 12:9.

Satan's and his demons have deceived some people on this earth to follow him; others just refused to repent to God, Revelation 13:14 and 16:11.

Hell is a place of immense torment with fire of brimstone which represents the immortal spirit burning for their sins that where committed on earth and refusing to follow or repent to God, Revelation 19:20.

The spirit's torment is so unbearable they weep in extreme pain their teeth gnash (grind), Luke 13:28.

For eternity, this immortal spirit suffers for being a non-believer or being un-repented for their sins.

As we can see there will be exceedingly great happiness and praise in the third Heaven than in hell, it is our choice where we decide we want to spend eternity, because it is going to be one or the other, there is no waiting room. We need to decide before we die because once our voices are silent it's DONE!

OBEDIENCE

Obedience is following the word and will of God.

I, myself, am an example, I had put off writing this book for some time, wasn't for sure if this is what I was supposed to be doing but through obedience I'm still writing for three years now making sure that what God has for me to express will be concise to the reader of this book.

Why is it so hard for us to obey anyone especially God, is it just our human nature alone? As a youth, not obeying our parents seemed like a rite of passage to adulthood. When it comes to Our Father, God, do we want to treat him the way we treated our earthly parents? Remember God has a heaven and hell to put in unlike our earthly parents.

Jesus obeyed the Father, by laying down his life for us though he asked:

Mark 14:36

> "Abba Father, all things are possible for You, take this cup away from Me; neither the less, not what I will but what You will." NKJV

What makes us so much better than Jesus, having the nerve to defy the will of God; he is only asking us to do what is best for us.

We will find any excuse to not obey, it will never lead to salvation nor will it benefit us in the long run to eternal life with God the Father.

Romans 5:19, one man's disobedience many were sinners, also by one's man's obedience many will be made righteous.

One man's disobedience:

Adam and Eve ate the fruit from the tree of life in the Garden of Eden, when God told them not to do so, but Satan tempted Eve, who ate first and then she gave to Adam, because of this action sin came upon the earth, Genesis 3:2-6.

One Man's obedience:

Jesus obeyed the Father; through his actions of obedience we can be saved:

John 6:38-40

> *"For I came down from heaven, not to do My own will, but the will of Him who sent me.*
>
> *This is the will of the Father, who sent Me, that all of He has given Me I should lose nothing, but should raise it up at the last day.*
>
> *And this is the will of Him who sent Me that everyone who sees the Son and believes in Him may have everlasting life, and I will raise him up at the last day."*
> NKJV

Jesus was saying that he only came to do the will of God and not for himself, giving all honor to the Father.

DISOBEDIENCE

Disobedience: when God asked his people to do his will and they don't do it, this is called being disobedient.

God wants us to follow him because he knows it benefits us but if we choose not to do it then we are not doing ourselves any favors.

Romans 10:21 God says to the children of Israel,

> "All day long I have stretched out My hands to a disobedience and contrary people." NKJV

God is always waiting for us to reach out to him.

1ˢᵗ Timothy 1: 9, Paul tells Timothy, one of his young ministers, that the law is not for those you choose to do right but for the ones that choose not to do right, the unholy, disobedient and those that do evil towards others these things are contradictive to the laws of God.

These people choose to live unholy lives.

Titus 3:3, teaches that we were once foolish, disobedient, deceivers, and serving our own desires in living a sinful life. We also showed hatefulness towards others from jealousy to pride.

As we can see, disobedience towards God is a foolish attempt to lead our own lives, which will cause us to fail and can lead us to destruction.

Psalm 50:22, those who forget God, he will tear them into pieces without a rescue from any one.

RIGHTEOUSNESS

Righteousness is obtained through faith, believing in Jesus Christ.

Matthew 5: 6, we should long to be filled with the righteousness of Jesus Christ which can fill us up in our walk for salvation.

Luke 1:75, we should show godliness and righteousness before God all the days we are on this earth.

Acts 10:35, every person in this world has the ability to revere and show uprightness towards God, for he will acknowledge us.

Romans 1:17, we gain faith through the righteousness of God as we live by faith.

Romans 5:17, the first man disobedience caused death to come upon the earth and it ruled it, but because of Jesus, he has given grace and righteousness to those who choose to receive it, grace and righteousness will rule for life.

Romans 10:10; believing in our heart and confess with our voice leads to righteousness that is made to salvation.

1st Peter 2:24, Jesus died for our sins on a cross, because of his stripes we are healed, and we can live in righteousness.

1st John 2:29, Jesus is righteous, and we who practice righteousness; we are born of him.

Jesus Christ redeemed us back to the Father through his death, burial and the resurrection and we may now gain righteousness by believing, trusting, and having faith in God through his son.

James 3:18, if we have peace within ourselves and then demonstrate peace with others this creates the fruit of righteousness.

SALVATION

Salvation is being saved through Jesus Christ; we can be saved if we believe in his death, burial, and resurrection.

John 3:16, Jesus says,

> "For God so loved the world that He gave His only begotten Son, that whoever believes in Him should not perish but have everlasting life." NJKV

Luke 1:76-77,

> "And you child, will be called the prophet of the Highest; for you will go before the face of the Lord to prepare His way,
>
> To give knowledge of salvation to His people, by the remission of their sins," NKJV

This scripture takes place where Elizabeth had given birth to a son, John the Baptist, and her husband was filled with the Holy Spirit after she had given birth and he gave thanks to God for the blessing he had brought forth in the linage of their family history, descendants of King David.

Acts 13:26, Paul was teaching the people sitting with him, the ministry of John the Baptist and told them his of foreseeing of Jesus, who, was to be the salvation for the world.

Philippians 2:12, Paul was telling the believers in Philippi to continue to be followers of the truth in Jesus Christ and they should continue even in his absence; to acknowledge the salvation within them with honor and joy.

John 10:28-30 Jesus said,

> "And I give unto them eternal life; and they shall never perish, neither shall any man pluck them out of my hand.
>
> My Father, which gave them me, is greater than all; and no man is able to pluck them out of my Father's hand.
>
> I and my Father are One." KJV

No one loses salvation once it is gained, Hebrew 6:4-6, though one can doubt which leads to them doubting their salvation is a personal spiritual notion of the individual which is not truly lost but only in the their thinking because their acts or deeds that go against God is their reason for thinking salvation is lost.

A person's work or deeds does not make them gain salvation (Ephesians 2:8-9), but only believing in Jesus Christ leads to Salvation which is a personal spiritual choice, if one decides to stop believing in Jesus Christ then salvation is truly lost.

REDEMPTION

Redemption is the action of being saved from an error or wrong doing; this is the reason why Jesus came to earth.

Through Jesus' blood we were redeemed back to the Father by the sacrificial lamb that was sent to die for our sins.

Hebrews 9:11-15

> *"But Christ came as High Priest of the good things to come, with the greater and more perfect tabernacle not made with hands that is, not of this creation.*
>
> *Not with the blood of goats and calves, but with His own blood He entered the Most Holy Place once for all, having obtained eternal redemption.*
>
> *For it the blood of bulls and goats and the ashes of a heifer, sprinkling the unclean, sanctifies for the purifying of the flesh,*
>
> *How much more shall the blood of Christ, who through the eternal Spirit offered Himself without spot to God, cleanse your conscience from dead works to serve the living God?*

And for this reason, He is the Mediator of the new covenant, by means of death, for the redemption of the transgressions under the first covenant that those who are called may receive the promise of the eternal inheritance." NKJV

Before Jesus, animal's blood (goats, sheep, and bulls) were used as a sacrifice for sins of the people, 2^nd^Chronicles 29:21.

Hebrews 13:11, the high priest brought the blood of the animals into the sanctuary for sin, but the animals' bodies were burned outside the camp.

Jesus was the last sacrifice needed to redeem us back to the Father, through the shedding of his blood on the cross we can now go to God in prayer and asking in Jesus name, to forgive us of our sins if we sincerely desire to be forgiven.

Ephesians 1:7, through Jesus we are redeemed because the blood he shed which forgives sin and because of the righteousness of his grace.

REPENTANCE

Repentance is being remorseful or full of regret for being disobedient to the will of God; no one can come to God without repenting of their sins.

1st Samuel 16:7 God spoke to Samuel "Do not consider his appearance or his height, for I have rejected him. The Lord does not look at the things people look at. People look at the outward appearance, but God the Lord looks at the heart."

If your prayer of forgiveness is sincere God will know, people may or may not hear your confession but God cannot be deceived for he sees beyond what people see and hear.

Acts 8:22, sincerely pray and repent from our hearts for our wickedness, perhaps God will forgive if the sincerity is true.

2nd Timothy 2:25-26,

> "In humility correcting those who are in opposition, if God perhaps will grant them repentance, so that they may know the truth,
>
> And that they may come to their senses and escape the snare of the devil, having been taken captive by him to so his will." NKJV

We need to repent for our sins and be saved by recognizing we are sinners, as we pray and seek forgiveness.

Those that do not believe in praying and asking forgiveness have been fooled by the devil or their own way of thinking, are truly deceiving themselves in their thoughts which leads to nowhere good.

Hebrews 6:6, Paul is saying here, those who sin can be restored through repentance, however, Jesus is crucified and humiliated all over again for the sin they committed.

Basically, when you sin and you request forgiveness, your sin has still condemned Jesus to die again.

2nd Peter 3:9, the Lord doesn't slack for nothing in his promises, though some may think God is slacking, but with long-suffering he is not willing that not one on this earth should perish but come to God and repent for their sin.

Self-reflection: God is patient in waiting for all people to come to him through his Son, Jesus, that all may be saved through repentance. Where would we be if God wasn't patient?

GRACE

Grace is God's forgiving love:

Ephesians 2:5, though we were dead in our sins; but we are now made alive together with Christ; because we have been saved through his grace.

If we truly repent and turn away from sin, God's grace is so sweet we don't even have to work for it; it's given freely to those who truly are seeking forgiveness.

We have grace as believers and non-believers, God loves us all and grace is given not because we earned it but because of LOVE nothing more. We could have died in our sins, but by God's son Jesus we have grace and we should be grateful for this gift.

Self-reflection: As long as you live grace is given to you, are you going to acknowledge the gift you receive and thank God.

Ephesians 2:8, for it is by grace we are saved through faith, and not by our own doing but by the grace, the gift of God.

That is wonderful knowing God loves us that much and more; "Grace like Rain" is a beautiful song so true in its meaning, God's grace falls like rain covering all our sins; as we believe and trust in him.

James 4:6, God withstands the proud but grace is presented to those that are humble.

2nd Corinthians Chapter 12: Paul had a physical pain in his side, he was thinking it came from a messenger of Satan (7), and he requested to God to remove the pain from him 3 times (8) but God told Paul that *"My grace is sufficient for thee: for my strength is made perfect in weakness."* Paul then said *"Most gladly therefore will I rather glory in my infirmities that the power of Christ may rest upon me."* (9) KJV

Paul says;

> *"Therefore I take pleasure in infirmities in reproaches, in necessities, in persecutions, in distresses for Christ's sake: for when I am weak, then am I strong."*(10) KJV

Paul realized that he would gladly suffer with his pain with the strength of the God because in his weakness God is stronger within him.

MERCY

Mercy is having compassion for others.

Matthew 7:12, whatever we require of others to do for us, then we also do towards them for this is of law and by the Prophets.

Now a day, it doesn't seem like there is much mercy in the world, it literally has become a dog eat dog. If we would show more compassion for one another just think of how different this world would be. God has compassion for everyone even those that do not believe in him.

Racism has been on the rise since 2019 for people of color and for other nationalities here in the United States. Some people don't see others the way they see themselves.

Self-reflection: how can anyone think superiority is determined by the color of a person's skin and they can treat others based on that thinking?

If there was more mercy given in this world; color wouldn't matter but this world is not there in the wake of what is happening.

I mentioned earlier about the Coronavirus and now the vaccines are being administered, and I see that God is no longer being mentioned as when it first began.

People were praying on news channels, some religious leaders were speaking publicly, and it seemed people were leaning on God for help. But now, all you see are doctors talking about the break-through in vaccines and how it can contain the virus.

No one is saying God has given them the ability to provide vaccines but pharmaceutical companies are patting themselves on their backs for finding a way to help combat the virus. I see that my earlier statement is true man gets the credit and God doesn't exist anymore in the minds of men (human beings).

I know you may think that racism and the CoVid19 pandemic doesn't seem to have anything to do with mercy but it does, how?

Well first of all, we should have mercy for every human being on this earth regardless of color, creed, nationalities, gender, beliefs, life styles, or other ways people discriminate against others.

People do not choose the color of their skin the creator does, God. In the beginning, God said all the things he created are good so that tells us that no matter what color we are; we are good and there is no favoritism in God's sight, Genesis 1:31

At the time I wrote this book, the vaccines seemed to be distributed based on economic or social basis. Some news channels have stated that there is a limited amount of vaccines going to certain communities in the United States.

In these two instances, there seems to be no mercy towards others, hate and separation of economic status can keep one from showing mercy.

As of July 2021, some people were hesitating on taking the vaccines which may or may not have caused an upswing in Covid cases in some states. Though this may not seem to be in the topic of mercy in a sense, but this is proof in asking are people thinking of others or just being selfish? Well this was great debate at the time, see how this fits into mercy.

Remember when the pandemic first hit, people were upset about having to wear a mask and later on people were upset about taking the vaccine. We as a people are so fickle that we don't know what we will argue for or against, what is best or not?

God could kill us all if he wanted to like in Noah's time with flooding of the earth or destroying cities like he did with Sodom and Gomorrah, Genesis 7:17-24 and 19:24-25, respectively.

Self-reflection: Wow, think about that, God could kill us all if he wanted to but the mercy he has for us truly exceeds and ascends all aspect of the human mind. Isn't it so amazing how wonderful God is to us?

Do we really deserve so much of what God has given us at this or any other time?

REVERENCE

Reverence is giving honor, showing fear, adoration, worshiping, and offering a deep respect to someone or something.

Deuteronomy 4:10, Moses was speaking to the Israelites reminding them to continue to remember all they had seen, that God had done for them and let it not depart from them. Telling them to give God reverence for when they left Horeb to go the land God provided and promised to them. Also they needed to tell their children and their children's children to give honor to God all the days of their lives.

Psalm 111:9, King David was mentioning that God had redeemed his chosen people, the Israelites, and his covenant is commanded towards them forever, therefore, his name should be acknowledged with holiness and reverence.

There is nothing or no one above God; for he is a jealous God:

Exodus 34:14, we should worship no other God and because God is a jealous God, for his name is Jealous.

God's glory will not be given to anyone or anything that he has created.

As the creator of the world, reverence is owed to GOD!!

NAMES OF GOD

God has many names based the actions he performs and calling out his name is a good indication of who he is for us in our times of need.

These scriptures were taken from the NKJV:

Yahweh: The self-existent One:

Genesis 2:4

> *"This is the history of the heavens and the earth when they were created, in the day that the Lord God made the earth and the heavens."*

Adonai: Lord, Master:

Deuteronomy 10:17

> *"For the Lord, your God is God of gods, and Lord of lords, the great God, mighty and awesome, who shows no partially not takes a bribe."*

Attiyq Youm: The Ancient of Days, God is Eternal:

Daniel 7: 9, 13-14

"I watched till thrones were put in place and the Ancient of Days was seated; His garment was white as snow, and the hair of His head was like pure wool, His throne was a fiery flame, its wheels a burning fire,

I was watching in the night visons, and behold, One like the Son of Man coming with the clouds of heaven! He came to the Ancient of Days and they brought Him near and before Him.

Then to Him was given dominion and glory and a kingdom that all peoples, nations, and languages should serve Him. His dominion is an everlasting dominion, which shall not pass away, and His kingdom the one which shall not be destroyed."

El – Elyon: The Most High:

Isaiah 14:13-14

"For you have said in your heart: I will ascend into heaven, I will exalt my throne above the stars of God; I will also sit on the mount of the congregation, on the farthest sides of the north;

I will ascend above the heights of the clouds; I will be like the Most High."

Elohim: God's Power and Might:

Jeremiah 31:33

> "But this the covenant that I will make with the house of Israel after those days, says the Lord, I will put My law in their minds and write it on their hearts, and I will be their God and they shall be My people."

El-Gibhor: Mighty God:

Isaiah 9:6

> "For unto us a child is born. Unto us a Son is given. And the government will be upon his shoulder. And His name will be called Wonderful, Counselor, Mighty God, Everlasting Father, and Prince of Peace."

El-Olam: The Everlasting God:

Isaiah 40:28-31

> "Have you not known? Have you not heard? The everlasting God, the Lord. The Creator end of the earth neither faints nor is weary, His understanding is unsearchable.
>
> He gives power to the weak, And to those who have no might He increases strength,
>
> Even the youths shall faint and be weary, and the young men shall utterly fall,
>
> But those who wait on the Lord Shall renew their strength; they shall mount up with wings like eagles;

they shall run and not be weary, they shall walk and not faint."

El-Roi: The strong who sees:

Genesis 16:13

"Then she called the name of the Lord who spoke to her, You are The God who Sees, for she said, Have I also here seen Him who sees me?"

El-Shaddai-Rohi: God Almighty:

Genesis 17:1

"When Abram was ninety-nine years old, The Lord appeared to Abram and said to him, I am Almighty God; walk before Me and be blameless."

El- Chuwl: The God who gave birth:

Psalm 139:13-18

"For You formed my inward parts, You covered me in my mother's womb.

I will praise You, for I am fearfully and wonderfully made; marvelous are Your works, and that my soul knows very well.

My frame was not hidden from You, when I was made in secret, and skillfully wrought in the lowest parts of the earth.

Your eyes saw my substance being yet informed and in Your book they all were written, the days fashioned for me, When as yet there were none of them.

How precious also are Your thoughts to me, O God! How great is the sum of them!

If I should count them, they would be more in number than the sand, When I awake, I am still with You."

El-Deah: God of knowledge:

Romans 11:33-36

"Oh, the depth of the riches both of the wisdom and knowledge: of God! How unsearchable are His judgments and His ways past finding out!

For who has known the mind of the Lord? Or who has become His counselor?

Or who has first given to Him and it shall be repaid to him?

For of Him and through Him and to Him are all things, to whom be glory forever. Amen"

Yahweh – Maccaddeshem: The Lord your sanctifier:

Leviticus 20:8

"And you shall keep My statutes and perform them: I am the Lord who sanctifies you."

Yahweh Rohi: The Lord is my Shepard:

Jeremiah 31:10

> *"Hear the word of the Lord, O nations, and declare it in the isles afar off and say, He who scattered Israel will gather him, and keep him as a Shepard does his flock."*

Yahweh-Shammah: The Lord is present:

Amos 5:14

> *"Seek good and not evil, that you may live, so the Lord God of hosts will be with you, as you have spoken."*

Yahweh-Rapha: The Lord our healer:

2ⁿᵈ Chronicles 7:14

> *"If my people who are called by name will humble themselves and pray and seek My face and turn from their wicked ways then I will hear from heaven and will forgive their sin and heal their land."*

Yahweh-Tsidkenu: The Lord our righteousness:

Genesis 15:6

> *"And he believed in the Lord, and He accounted it to him for righteousness."*

Yahweh Jireh: The Lord will provide:

Genesis 22: 13-14

"Then Abraham lifted his eyes and looked and there behind him was a ram caught in a thicket by its horn. So Abraham went and took the ram, and offered it up for a burnt offering instead of his son.

And Abraham called the name of the place, The Lord Will Provide as it is said to this day in the Mount of the Lord it shall be provided."

Yahweh-Nissi: The Lord our banner:

Exodus 17: 15-16

"And Moses built an altar and called its name The Lord Is My Banner,"

For he said "Because the Lord has sworn: the Lord will have war with Amalek from generation to generation."

Yahweh-Shalom-The Lord is peace:

Judges 6:24

"So Gideon built an altar there to the Lord and called it The Lord Is Peace. To this day it is still in Oprah of the Abiezrites."

Yahweh–Sabbaoth: The Lord of Hosts:

1st Samuel 17:45

"Then David said to the Philistine, You come to me with a sword, with a spear, and with a javelin. But I come to you in the name of the Lord of hosts, the God of the armies of Israel, whom you have defied."

Yahweh-Ghmolah: The God of Recompense:

Jeremiah 51:6

> *"Flee from the mist of Babylon and every one save his life! Do not be cut off in her iniquity for this is the time of the Lord's vengeance He shall recompense her."*

THREE ARE ONE

God, Jesus and the Holy Spirit are one, some will truly lose me on this topic, but please try to stay with me; I know God is doing this work in me to put this out there for true knowledge not to cause conflict but to understand the concept of 3 are 1. God said in the beginning of creation;

Genesis 1:26

> *"Let Us make man in Our image...."* NIV

Jesus and the Holy Spirit were there because God used the word *"Us"* we know from attending elementary school *"us"* means more than one.

John 1:1

> *"In the beginning was the Word, and the Word was with God, and the Word was God."* NIV

John 1:14, Jesus is the Word that became flesh and lived among the people.

See the Word is capitalized meaning Jesus is the Word that was God, and with God, and became flesh.

John 10:30, Jesus stated that He and the Father are one.

1st John 5:7, there are three in heaven that bear witness, the Father; God, the Word who is Jesus and the Holy Spirit, for these three are one.

So now with these scriptures in mind, imagine God, Jesus, and the Holy Spirit as one entity. Think of it like three people dancing in a choreography, in sync with one another in style and rhythm, being on one accord; having all things in common.

Performing in a formation where we only see one but the others are there. That is actually how God, Jesus and the Holy Spirit work, flowing in motion that looks like one spiritual being but there are 3.

This is the interpretation of what God has given me to rely to you, God, Jesus, and the Holy Spirit working so beautifully in line with the love, grace, and mercy for us, it flows as a beautiful wave like on the ocean so amazing to see such a dance that they perform for us daily.

Letting us know they are covering, watching, and desiring us as one of their own.

STRENGTH

Strength is enduring and pushing through rough situations or circumstances with everything that is in us. We can all use so much more strength at this time, right?

So how does strength relate to us when it comes to God?

Well, when Jesus was in the Garden of Gethsemane praying he was weak in his flesh, but not in the spirit, asking for physical strength from the Father to help him endure what was before him, Matthew 26:39.

Jesus asked for strength for the beatings, piercing of his side, and being hung on a cross, that was to come, through God's strength he was able to fulfill his Father purpose to die so we could be redeemed back to God.

We also get our strength from God or did you think you were doing it all by yourself, WRONG.

As people, we are weak and need God to give us the strength to endure daily living. We ask in prayer, for God to strengthen our mind, body, and spirit, because they are being attacked daily from sun up to sun down in all faucets of our lives.

Psalm 84:5-7

> *"Blessed is the man whose strength is in You, Whose heart is set on pilgrimage,*
>
> *As they pass through the Valley of Baca They make it a spring; the rain also covers it with pools.*
>
> *They go from strength to strength each one appears before God in Zion."* NKJV

King David was giving praise to God for the strength he provided while making the pilgrimage to the temple in the Holy City, Jerusalem.

King David knew where he received his strength it came from God.

Previously mentioned, 2nd Corinthians 12:9, Paul asked God to heal his infirmity but God told Paul that in his pain the strength that He provides would endure through Paul's weakness; God's grace was Paul's strength.

So no matter how weak we may be physically, mentally or spiritually God provides strength to help us endure.

MEDITATION

Meditating on God's word and seeking guidance would be a delight for our spirit and not relying on our own thinking which can lead to self-destruction.

Psalm 1:1-2

> "Blessed is the man that walketh not in the counsel of the ungodly, nor standeth in the way of sinners, nor sitteth in the seat of the scornful.
>
> But his delight is in the law of the Lord; and in his law doth he meditate day and night." KJV

The more we put God's words in us, the more we will be able to speak his words to any situation or circumstances that will occur. The words will come to our remembrance as Jesus did when he was tempted by the devil (Matthew 4:1-11).

So make and take time to read God's word (The Holy Bible) to seek his guidance.

The body needs food and water to stay healthy; meditating quietly on God's word will allow letting his words to soak into us.

The body will be rejuvenated and refreshed when meditating on God's word, because it allows us to be able to endure life challenges with just a verse or scriptures that will come to remembrance, and to speak to any situation or circumstance in Jesus' name.

Psalm 77:11-14

> "I will remember the works of the Lord; surely I will remember Your wonders of old.
>
> I will also meditate also on all Your work, and talk to your deeds.
>
> Your way, O God is in the sanctuary; who is so great a God as our God?
>
> You are the God who does wonders: You have declared Your strength among the people." NKJV

SPIRIT

The spirit is the eternal or inner being in us, believers and non-believers, this spirit returns back to God for judgment, Revelation chapter 20.

Paul said;

Romans 7:21-24

> "So I find this law at work: Although, I want to do good evil is right there with me.
>
> For in my inner being I delight in God's law,
>
> But I see another law at work in me waging war against the law of my mind and making me a prisoner of the law of sin at work within me.
>
> What a wretched man that I am! Who will rescue me from this body that is subject to death?" NIV

We should, as Paul says, desire to do the right things and desire our inner-spirits to commune with God; but we also have the sinful nature too, we must submit ourselves to God's will and fight against doing wrong, only with the help of God can we defeat our sinful ways.

Don't get this confused with the Holy Spirit, which is the third Godhead, this particular spirit I am referring to in this topic was given to man when he created the first man, Adam, Genesis 2:7.

The use of the word spirit and soul have been used interchangeably in the scriptures (Genesis 41:8, Psalms 42:6, John 12:27 and 13:21), but Hebrew 4:12 gives a distinction between spirit and soul.

"For the word of God is living and powerful, and sharper than any two-edged sword, piercing even to the division of soul and spirit, and of joints and marrow, and is a discerner of the thoughts and intents of the heart."
NKJV

It has been said that the spirit is heavenly while the soul is considered earthly.

THE HOLY SPIRIT

This is the third of the Godhead (God, Jesus). This is God's power in action, (Luke 1:35)

Before Jesus ascended into Heaven to return to the father, he gave his disciples instructions to go and wait for the Holy Spirit to come upon them and continue to do the work of the ministry, bringing people to God through him, Jesus Christ. (Acts chapter 1 and 2).

The Holy Spirit only identifies with the Spirit of God in a person, where God does not dwell the Holy Spirit does not recognize, (Romans 8:9).

The Holy Spirit is the promise or guarantee to those who have chosen to follow God and his instructions, they will receive the inheritance of eternal life being redeemed from sin, Ephesians 1:13-14.

The Holy Spirit provides gift to baptized believers to edify and strengthen the churches of God.

The spiritual gifts and churches are mentioned later in the book.

FRUITS OF THE SPIRIT

Fruits of the spirit are: love, joy, peace, long-suffering, gentleness, goodness, faith, meekness, and temperance......, Galatians 5:22-23

We can see how, God is love on a daily basis as he allows us to see the wonders of this world, changing of the seasons, birds of the air, animals on land and in the sea, feel the wind blowing in our hair or in the trees, sun shining on our faces, moon glowing, stars twinkling, and so much more seen and unseen.

Self-reflection: as human beings, breathing is love from God we are not doing it on our own, if you think otherwise Sorry NO!!!

Without giving it a single thought we go on about our daily lives taking God's pure love for granted.

The First greatest Commandment: Jesus spoke,

> *"We shall love the Lord your God with all your heart, with all your soul, with all your mind, and with all your strength."*

And the Second greatest Commandment:

> *"You shall love your neighbor as yourself."* Mark 12:30-31, NKJV

Self-reflection: If we love God with everything that is in us, then we could treat others the way we want to be treated. It would be a lot less hate in this world today.

We have all we have because of God's love, he gave it to us, all of us and that is wonderful to know, however, without his love we wouldn't even be here.

LOVE

There are 4 types of love: Storge (family), Philia (friendship), Eros (physical), and Agape (Godly):

Storge is showing love towards mom, dad, siblings, and other family members, this love is unforced, just comes naturally, like brothers growing up together forming storge love between their parents and themselves, Romans 12:10.

Parents should love their children unconditionally but it not always the case and it didn't always happen automatically, for some the relationship begins before the child is born and can stay bound even after death.

Some family members can hold on to grudges that last for days or even years and the situation never gets resolved breaking the family apart. God can bless and restore the storge love if members humble themselves and seek forgiveness from one another to bring back the wholeness of the family.

But some people are just determined to be unhappy with their family; they don't even attend special or sad occasions because of the hurt. But God heals the heart and strengthen the love once again if they are willing to submit to him in their hurt and pain. God knows a healthy family is a strong family as long as he is the foundation.

Philia is showing brotherly love to friends and acquaintances we come in contact; the disciples showed philia to one another and to other baptized believers during the time of Pentecost, Acts chapter 2.

Paul showed philia love when he was in prison towards the guards, Acts 16: 25-40.

Paul performed philia love when corresponding to the churches, sending greetings to them in Rome, Corinth, Galatia, Ephesus, Philippi, Colossae, and Thessalonica.

Paul and the disciples considered every person whom they were teaching about the word of God, a brother through Christ Jesus.

Jesus received everyone as a brother or sister according to his Father, Matthew 12:47-50.

1st Samuel 1:4, David was a close friend to Jonathan whose father (Saul) was king at the time and he wanted to kill David because he was to become the next king.

1st Samuel 18:1-4, Jonathan loved David and they made a covenant, Johnathan gave David his robe, garments, and his sword this action showed David that Johnathan saw him as a brother as an heir to the throne.

1st Samuel 20:16-17, again Jonathan made a covenant with David cause of the love he had for him.

Self-reflection: How would the world be if we had the philia love towards others?

Strangers are friends we haven't met yet!

Eros is romantic, sensual, and physical love meant to be between a husband and his wife, when God created Adam and Eve, he desired their love to be only to each other, and no one could take one from the other, Genesis 3:16

It was God plan that a man stayed with his wife and vice versa until death, but when sin came upon the earth man's heart changed but God's plan didn't.

When the hearts of man changed the feelings towards their spouse changed, the men removed the women they no longer desired from their homes; Deuteronomy 24:1-2.

The man would give the woman a certificate of divorce and puts her out of his house, when she leaves and becomes another man's wife.

Jesus stated in Matthew 5:31-32;

> *"Furthermore it has been said; whoever divorces his wife let him give her a certificate of divorce.*
>
> *But I say to you, that whoever divorces his wife for any reason except for sexual immortality causes her to commit adultery; and whoever marries a woman who is divorced commits adultery."* NKJV

A man is supposed to leave his mother and father and cleave to his wife and they become one letting no man pull them apart, Matthew 19:5-6.

Jesus told the people that because the hardening of man's (human) heart Moses wrote a certificate of divorce but in the beginning this was not supposed to be so, Mark 10:4-9.

Jesus says;

> *"Whoever divorces his wife and marries another; commits adultery against her.*

And if a woman divorces her husband and marries another, she commits adultery." (11-12) NKJV

A broken commandment, we should not commit adultery, but sins can be forgiven:

1st John 1:9, if we confess our sins, God is faithful, willing to forgive, and clean us from all unrighteousness.

Agape is the Godly love, it's unconditional and universal; Jesus is the perfect example of agape love in the flesh. He sacrificed himself to save and redeem the world back to the Father, through his death, burial, and resurrection.

Jesus showed this love to the world, but the world did not respond in kind towards him. However, he continued expressing agape love while knowing he must give his life so others may be saved. Jesus sacrificed himself for those that hated, whipped, mocked, spit, nailed and pierced him, Mark 15: 15-20, and 24.

But Jesus' love never swayed; through it all, Luke 23:34.

We need to follow Jesus examples and show agape love to everyone we meet. Just say a "Hello" or show a smile, or even say "Jesus loves you", showing love in a pleasing manner is also pleasing to God.

Showing agape love, even when there is no response in return, can dishearten us, don't get upset or mad if that happens; we will never know what that person may feel later or they may even say it to someone else because you choose to show them love first.

Self-reflection: little gestures such as these will also make you feel good that you can show love and allow God to help you express more agape love as you continue your walk with him.

JOY

Joy is an emotional characteristic that portrays a feeling of great happiness or gladness.

When reflecting on God and all he has done, joy should flow from you like rain pouring down during a strong thunder storm.

2nd Samuel 6:12-14

King David was in great joy for what God had done defeating his enemies and returning with the Ark of the Covenant (which contained the Ten Commandments God gave to Moses); David danced out of his clothes when he returned home.

There is so much we can receive when expressing joy, lifting up our hands, praising God with our voice in song, and rejoicing to him with such gladness it can over take us like David.

Being unhappy, mad, frustrated, angry, and upset are emotions that seem to drag us down, making us become depressed and defeated which can harm us spiritually but these things are not spirits of God, Colossians 3:5-9.

If we feel emotionally, mentally, physically and spiritually defeated we cannot have joy, we must run to the feet of God pour our heart out to him, by praying and crying out to him and giving him our troubles, then see if the joy doesn't come through, Psalm 61, 77,111, 120.

Luke 19:35-39

Jesus disciples were rejoicing as he was entering Jerusalem sitting on a colt, the disciples was acknowledging Jesus, as the King whom had come in the name of the Lord; and there was peace in heaven, and glory on high. The Pharisees requested that Jesus tell his disciples to stop shouting their remarks.

Self-reflection: If you have no desire to express joy for what God has done, is able to do and what he will do then, here is the outcome:

Luke 19:40 Jesus states;

> "I tell you that if these should keep silent, the stones would immediately cry out." NKJV

I'm not going to let an inanimate object cry out for me, I am going to give God glory by shouting and praising him for all he has done for me,

Self-reflection: are you going to do the same?

PEACE

Peace is the quietness of one's inner-man or inner-spirit, like when there is no wind, no animals making sounds outside, nothing flying in the air, just silent and still, that is the best I can describe peace but it's so much more than that.

Having peace is not letting anything disrupts us from what God has for our lives, but we can get frustrated and angry, peace can be overshadowed by the chaos and hassle of this life.

But we must seek peace in God by reflecting on his words, by finding the time to read scriptures or a verse on the issues that is disrupting our peace. Saying a little prayer wherever we are and speak to God to calm the storm within or around us.

The devil can disrupt our peace by taking away our joy, steal what God has for us, and destroy our spiritual mind.

John 10:10 Jesus says;

> "The thief cometh not, but for to steal, and to kill, and to destroy: I am come that they might have life, and they might have it more abundantly." KJV

When Jesus mentioned he came to give us life and that we may have it more abundantly, this abundance includes peace.

Isaiah 54:17 weapons created against us will not prosper, condemn all the tongues that come against us in judgment, this is our heritage and the righteousness of being servants of God, for the Lord had spoken.

So we are not going to let the devil or a person whom means us no good, to steal what is already given to us by God.

Philippians 4:7 God's peace will surpass all understanding; it will guard our minds and hearts through Jesus Christ.

We should leave our concerns and cares at God's feet, walk away knowing it is in his hands. Having faith, trusting, and not doubting, receiving peace and allowing it to grow, it will become a daily routine in our lives through Christ Jesus.

PATIENCE

Patience is the ability to tolerant situations or circumstances, without getting angry or becoming frustrated in any way. Patience comes before negativity; patience in the bible is also called steadfast.

We must have patience in order to endure this world as we continue to be led and guided by God.

Hebrews 10:36, after we have endured all on this earth and have done the will of God we may receive His promise.

The promise is **Eternal Life!**

We must also be patient with others, which I know at times is hard to do even more in this day and age, everyone wants something here and now. But being patient and showing compassion during this time when negativity can get the best of us is another step in spiritual growth.

James 1:3, understanding that the testing of our faith produces patience.

We need to increase our faith daily in order to increase patience in our lives.

So if we find ourselves in situation or circumstance that is trying to defeat us in our spiritual walk, just know that we can overcome by remaining calm and praying to God to give us strength to endure and he will see us through.

James 5:7-8

> "Therefore be patient, brethren until the coming of the Lord. See how the farmer waits for the precious fruit of the earth, waiting patiently for it until it receives the early and latter rain.
>
> You also be patient, establish your hearts for the coming of the Lord is at hand." NKJV

Self-reflection: as we are waiting patiently on the return of Jesus Christ, we must also show patience to every one we encounter in any situation.

LONG-SUFFERING

Long-suffering, which is manifested through patience, consents of self-control and forgiving one another.

Side note: Long-suffering is also considered forbearance, a delay of a repayment which is also found in the bible but I will not be referring to this definition.

Long-suffering being demonstrated through patience will allow us to be more Christ-like in every aspect of our lives.

James 1:19, Brothers and sisters take care to note that we should be quick to listen and slow to speak as well as slow to anger.

So when communicating with others we need to learn to listen more and speak less this will help us in our daily walk as children of God.

We need self-control in all aspects of our lives; we can't bring people to God when we are acting like the world.

John 15:19, Jesus says

> "If you belonged to the world, it would love you as its own; as it is you do not belong to the world, but I have chosen you out of the world, that is why the world hates you." NIV

God is setting us apart from the world, so we must be the salt of the earth showing patience and forgiving others.

Matthew 5:13 Jesus says;

> "You are the salt of the earth: but if the salt has loses it saltiness how can it be made salty again? It is longer good for anything except to be thrown out and trampled underfoot." NIV

Having self-control will help us contain our thoughts and actions so we can grow more in the will of God.

Question: Have you ever been in a situation that someone offended you or you offended someone, did you forgive them or vice versa?

These days the world is filled with so much hate, even looking at a person in an unintentional manner can lead to conflicts such as, name calling, cursing, and even worse violence.

Forgiving others can be hard for the carnal mind (flesh), but we as children of God should be the examples (salt of the earth) the world needs to follow in order to compel people to him. We need to forgive and look past others faults and flaws because no one is perfect on this earth.

Romans 3:10, there is no one that is righteous not one.

God did not make a mistake when he created us in his image, and we need to learn it is not our place to judge.

Matthew 7:1-2 NIV Jesus says,

> "Do not Judge or you too will be judged. For in the same way you judge others you will be judged and with the measure you use, it will be measured to you." NIV

Ok!!! Big hit to the brain, we must be mindful when we judge; for with the stick we use to judge others, it will be measured right back at us. Plus, we really don't have the time to judge anyone; we can't even correct our own faults and flaws on our own; and think we have the audacity try to tell someone about their issues.

Matthew 7:3-5 Jesus continued saying,

> "Why do you look at the speck of sawdust in your brother's eye, and pay no attention to the plank in your own eye?
>
> How can you say to your brother let me take the speck out your eye when all the time there is a plank in your own eye?
>
> You hypocrite, first take the plank out of your own eye and then you will see clearly to remove the speck from your brother's eye." NIV

Long-suffering displays patience which in turn will demonstrate self-control, forgiveness and becoming non-judgmental. We should try to work on being patience every day of our lives but again easier said than done, but as God continues to change our hearts and minds; we should not be judge and jury towards others when we cannot do anything for ourselves without God.

Long-suffering and patience are so entwined, can't be one without the other; while patience ensures our ability to wait, long-suffering ensures our ability to withstand all that we may come up against as we are patient with others and ourselves.

This is combination is how God is with us, he patiently waits for us to come to him and shows long-suffering for people to turn away from their own evil intentions that why we are still on this earth today because he is giving us a the chance to come to him before he takes our last breath.

GENTLENESS

Gentleness also requires us to be slow to speak and slow to anger, having compassion for everyone, not just with Christ like people; gentleness doesn't mean we are going to be push overs or show weakness, but gentleness is showing compassion for others in a way that we are putting others before ourselves; Jesus is our greatest role model.

James 1:19 we all should be quick to listen and slow to speak towards one another and also slow to cause anger.

Jesus was gentle towards the small children and to the older adults when he walked this earth. Jesus did not get frustrated when people did not believe in him or when he was talked about, he just continued on doing the will of His and Our Father.

Self-reflection: Being gentle to someone whom may have wronged us can be hard but know that Jesus endured being hated, talked about, beat, and crucified, so if he can show gentleness under those conditions why are we not able to be gentler in this world?

We can endure with the help of God; we need to rely on his strength when we are weak and in despair, God will provide his compassion and comfort towards us as we go through. We must not let people challenge or deter us from showing gentleness because it will benefit us in the end.

GOODNESS

Goodness, is having an upstanding character in action, words, or deed, no one needs to be perfect to be good, because no one is perfect. Goodness is showing kindness towards everyone not just the people around us.

Ecclesiastes 7:20, there is no human being on earth that does exceedingly good and does not sin.

Mark 10:18, Jesus asked,

> "Why do call me good? No one is good but one, that is God." NKJV

Everyone deserves to receive goodness whether they reciprocate it or not. Jesus showed goodness to those who rejected him when he returned home and also to those that wanted to kill him:

Mark 6:1-3

When Jesus returned to his hometown, Nazareth, he was speaking in the synagogue but no one there believed him and was offended with him,

Jesus said,

> "A prophet is not without honor, but in his own country and among his own kin, and in his own house." (4) KJV

After Jesus was betrayed by Judas and was arrested one the followers struck a soldier and cut off his right ear, Luke 22:47-49.

But Jesus answered saying *"suffer ye this far."* And he touched the soldier's ear and healed him. (51)

Jesus is TRULY the role model for us to show goodness towards everyone, even those who have wronged us.

Luke 6:27-29, Jesus says,

> *"But to you who are listening I say love your enemies, do good to those who hate you.*
>
> *Bless those who curse you, pray for those who mistreat you.*
>
> *If someone slaps you on one cheek, turn to them the other also. If someone takes your coat, do not withhold your shirt from them."* NIV

It may also be hard for us to love our enemies because we think they don't deserve our goodness, thinking it would be time wasted or unappreciated.

Thinking that type of way is wrong and we need to remove it from our thoughts; all of God's creations (believers and non-believers) deserve to be shown goodness.

Psalm 27:13, we could have lost heart unless we had believed in the goodness of the Lord for ourselves while we are alive.

Psalm 31:19, God goodness is so great that the abundance he has stored up for those who revere him; and God will present it in the sight of men for those who have a sanctuary in him.

FAITH

Faith is having trust and believing in God without doubt, within your heart, soul, mind and strength.

Self-reflection: though you might feel you can't fathom an outcome from a bad overwhelming situation or circumstance just trust in God.

Hebrews 11:1, truly having faith and believing that we hope for will come to fruition, even though we cannot see it.

God knows our every need and what is best for us; Jesus understands every issue we go through because he was tempted by the devil.

After spending 40 days and 40 nights; fasting, praying, and spending time with his Father.

Matthew 4:1-11, the devil, showed up to tempt the Lord when he thought Jesus was at his weakest.

Self-reflection: isn't that just like him (the devil), showing up when he feels we are at our lowest and in a vulnerable state in our lives.

But Jesus was able to use the word of God to defeat the devil's lies and deceptions because Jesus knew our Father's words were and are TRUE forever, TRUE.

The devil couldn't compel Jesus to defy God's will, for Jesus knew his purpose.

We need to follow Jesus' example though it may be the toughest thing not being able to see the light at the end of the tunnel in difficult times, but just knowing Jesus has gone ahead of us, hold on, trust and believe he has our back and he will see us through.

God allows us to go through situations or circumstances to strengthen our faith in him, if God rescued us every time we fell down and cleaned us up for our actions without any accountability towards others or ourselves would we have learned anything?

The Father will provide, protect, comfort, strengthen, guide, lead, and will do so much more, in the good times as well as the bad.

Self-reflection: do you think that all you do is without God? Why are you thinking so foolishly?

Galatians 6:3, if anyone thinks that all the abilities or talents they have is from them alone has deceived themselves in being foolish minded in thinking in such a manner.

God gives us the ability to perform the actions, talents and abilities we have today to become doctors, masonry workers, scientists and artists just for examples.

I know you have heard this before, why is God not helping people? Why are there diseases, disasters, unimaginable circumstances and situations in the world, if he can do what the bible said he did, why isn't he doing it now?

God allows these situations to arise to remind us he is in control and things happen for a reason, we won't understand why but he has a purpose and we must trust him.

I know for some people this answer isn't good enough but I can say there is a blessing in all that God does seen and unseen.

When we ask God to intervene when praying for family members, friends, and those that are suffering with illnesses or others who are going through difficult times, he will bless us with the request, but other times the results are not the answer we expected.

If a family member or friend passes away after praying for healing we may feel discouraged that God did not hear our prayer or that he did not want to heal them.

We must realize God answers all prayers that line up with his word, also God knows what he is doing and he will reveal the reason in his time.

In the book of John, chapter 11 (KJV); Jesus raised Lazarus:

Jesus had a friend named Lazarus, who was sick and his sisters sent men to ask for Jesus to come quickly to heal him. (3)

Jesus stated to the messengers *"This sickness is not unto death, but for the glory of God, that the Son of God might be glorified thereby."*(4)

Jesus loved this family and was two days away from the residents, he told his disciples they were headed to Judea, and that Lazarus is sleeping and we will go wake him up from his sleep. (5-11)

The disciples didn't quite figure out what Jesus meant hearing him say "sleeping". So Jesus told his disciples that *"Lazarus is dead"* and he was glad for their sakes that he was not there to heal Lazarus so they may believe so they must go to him now. (12-15)

When Martha, Lazarus' sister, heard Jesus was coming she went and meet him while the other sister, Mary stayed in the house. Martha wanted Jesus to know, if he had been here Lazarus wouldn't have died but what God allows his will be done. (21-22)

Jesus told Martha that *"her brother will rise again"* and Martha believed that Lazarus would rise again in the resurrection and Jesus told Martha, *"I am the resurrection and the life, he that believeth in me though he were dead, yet shall he live. And whosoever liveth and believeth in me shall never die. Believeth thou this?"* (23-26) KJV

Martha, believed Jesus is the Christ, the Son of God which came into the world. Martha left Jesus and returned to home to Mary to let her know that Jesus was coming and Mary went to him. Still distance away from the sister's home, Mary went to Jesus and fell at his feet. (32)

She repeated the same sentiments Martha had previously spoken to Jesus about their brother, Lazarus. When Jesus saw her weeping and the other mourners, he was groaned (grieved) in his spirit and was troubled. (33)

The Jesus asked *"where have ye laid him?"* (34)

When they arrived at the site grave Jesus wept. (35)

The mourners were thinking of how much Jesus must have loved Lazarus because he shed tears over his friend. (36)

Some questioned why Jesus let Lazarus die when he was able to make a blind man see. (37)

Jesus told them to *"take away the stone"*, Martha mentioned to Jesus that her brother has been dead for four days and that he would be stinking. Jesus said to her *"Said I not unto thee, that if thou wouldest believe, thou shouldest see the glory of God?"* (39-40) KJV

Once the stone was remove Jesus lifted up his eyes, and said *"Father, I thank thee that thou hast heard me. And I knew that thou hearest me always: but because of the people which stand by I said it, that they may believe that thou hast sent me."* (41-42)

Jesus, cried out in a loud voice; *"Lazarus come forth."*(43)

When he came forth he was bound hand, feet, with graves clothes, and his face was covered with a napkin. Jesus told the people to loosen him, and let him go. (44)

When Lazarus died, it was a great opportunity for the people to see that Jesus is truly the Son of God by raising Lazarus from the dead. Jesus saw their sorrow and for the compassion Jesus had towards mankind caused him to weep.

The other reason he wept was due to the people's unbelief that Jesus words he was speaking was about him. When Martha mentioned she believed that Jesus was the Christ, the Son of God, but to really believe it was questioned by the tears she shed in the pain of losing her brother.

The sisters and the mourners present at the tomb, truly didn't comprehend that the resurrection was in their midst.

We may or may not be aware that God is comforting us in our time of pain of losing a loved one or a friend and don't quite understand why God took them home, he is trying to get our attention, but in that moment of sadness we are not trying to hear God.

But as always God is showing us he is in control and that no matter what he does it benefits us and gives him glory, so we must trust in God even when going through the pain of loss.

Pain doesn't last always and finding the comfort in God is easier said than done, I know, we all know; but in his time, God's reason for what or why we go through will be revealed.

In any situation or circumstances, we have to remember who we are and whose we are; children of God and God's children.

Galatians 3:26, we all are sons and daughter of God through Jesus Christ.

1st Timothy 6:12, endure the good fight of faith which will lead to eternal life, as we having confessed and acknowledged the good admissions in attendance of plenty observers.

Let our faith guide us through difficult times in our lives as we become witnesses to others as we hold on to our faith, for in the end is eternal life.

2nd Corinthians 5:7, we are guided by our faith not by what we see.

MEEKNESS

Meekness is the attribute to gentleness, if we show gentleness; meekness will follow right along, not causing someone to be in pain or doing harm.

Gentleness is the words and meekness is the actions; our attitudes can be improved when showing both of the characteristics.

Remember all of us (human beings) are God's creation (saved and unsaved), no exceptions to the rule.

Titus 3:2, slander no one but show peace, consideration to all, and always show gentleness towards everyone.

1st Timothy 6:11, believers of God, flee from sin and follow after God whom shows righteousness, godliness, faith, love, patience and meekness.

Paul was saying flee from things that are not of God and things that are not good for us spiritually but follow after what God provides us.

Matthew 5:5 Jesus says,

"Blessed are the meek for they will inherit the earth." NIV

TEMPERANCE

Temperance is another aspect of self-control, while other fruits of the spirit affect us spiritually towards others this one is mainly personal, which can affect you spiritually; its characteristic is the lust of the flesh.

1st John 2:16, in this world, there is the lust of the flesh, eyes, and pride of life these do not come from God.

This is how temperance is personal I cannot tell you what you can or cannot do to your own body, but be mindful of how you use your body because it is where the spirit of God dwells and when you are following him you don't want to have a unclean (sin) attribute that can cause you to be apart from God. The lust of the flesh amounts to nothing in the end and you might get something you do not want.

Self-reflection: our bodies are temples to the Lord, so how we treat it affects the spirit within us, God cannot dwell in an unclean temple.

1st Corinthians 3:16-17

> "Don't you know that you yourselves are God's temple
> and that God's Spirit dwells in your midst?

If anyone destroys God's temple, God will destroy that person; for God's temple is sacred, and you together are that temple." NIV

Self-reflection: Try to work on the things or issues that could cause you to fall, and if you do, which we all will, repent and ask God to strengthen that area of weakness so your flesh or the devil cannot tempt you to fall again.

PHYSICAL AND SPIRITUAL BAPTISM

A physical baptism is symbolic gesture of being a child of God. After repenting and confessing that we believe that Jesus died, was buried and rose with all power and authority given to him by God; one can show publicly that they have made the commitment to follow God through Jesus Christ.

Being baptized requires the person to be immersed in water as Jesus' death, burial, and when raised out of the water as the symbolic gesture of his resurrection.

Mark 1:10, when John the Baptist, baptized Jesus, he came straight up out of the water.

Romans 6:4

> "Therefore we were buried with Him though baptism into death, that just Christ was raised from the dead by the glory of the Father, even so we also should walk in the newness of life."

> "For if we have been united together in the likeness of His death, certainly, we also shall be in the likeness of His resurrection" (5)

"Knowing this, that our old man was crucified with Him that the body of sin might be done away with, that we should no longer be slave of sin" (6) NKJV

A Spiritual baptism is the inward decision to surrender to the will of God and become part of the body of Christ.

Matthew 3:11, John the Baptist was telling the people that he was baptizing with water but the one coming after him will baptize them in the Holy Spirit and fire.

John 20:21-23 Jesus said;

"Peace to you! As the Father has sent Me, I also send you.

And when He had said this, He breathed on them, and said to them. Receive the Holy Spirit,

If you forgive the sins of any, they are forgiven them; if you retain the sins of any, they are retained." NKJV

Jesus commanded the disciples to not depart from Jerusalem but to wait for the Promise of the Father, he reminded the disciples that he had previously mentioned this to them:

Acts 1:5 Jesus says,

"For John truly baptized with water, but you shall be baptized with the Holy Spirit not many days from now."

The disciples ask Jesus if this was time of his coming to restore the kingdom of Israel. (6)

Jesus said to them verse 7 and 8,

> "It is not for you to know times or seasons which the Father has put in His own authority.
>
> But you shall receive power when the Holy Spirit has come upon you; and you shall be witnesses to Me in Jerusalem, and in all Judea and Samaria, and to the end of the earth." NKJV

The disciples thought Jesus had come back to claim the world as his Kingdom, which was to come, but Jesus had to inform the disciples that it was not for him to say but only his our father knows when Jesus will be returning to pronounce the Kingdom of God.

But instead Jesus was informing the disciples, that the Holy Spirit would be coming upon them soon and give them instructions.

This spiritual baptism is speaking in tongue is mentioned in this book.

LORD IS MY SHEPARD

Psalms 23 is a personal psalm or song of King David to God, acknowledging what God means to him and we can use it also in our daily lives.

"The Lord is my Shepard, I shall not want.

He makes me lie down in green pastures: he leads me beside the still waters,

He restores my soul: he leads me in the paths of righteousness for his name sake.

Yea, though I walk through the valley of the shadow of death, I fear no evil: For you are with me; your rod and your staff they comfort me.

You have prepared a table for me in the presence of mine enemies: you anointed my head with oil, my cup runs over.

Surely goodness and mercy shall follow me all the days of my life: and I will dwell in the house of the Lord forever." NKJV

Everything we need God gives, he is our Shepard, whom provides; like a pastor of sheep, for example, we are protected, cared and loved. God guides us in the way in which he wants us to go, through him we can and will be saved.

Though we may go through some tough times that may seem like darkness, God is with us, always protecting us with his rod and guiding us with his staff.

Even when our enemies come against us God shows honors towards us. He will see us through in times of trouble.

Remember, being God's children, we can rejoice and give honor to him for all he has and will do and in the end, we will live in Heaven for all eternity!!!

God's word is the rod and God's will is the staff

PRAYING

When we pray we are expressing thanks and requesting God to assist in an issue or situation.

Praying to God is a way to communicate with him personally by spiritually communicating with him.

Being baptized believers we know that God can aid in any situation that will arise in our lives. Praying to God for his help is showing him we trust and believe that he is the only one that can fix the problem.

Proverbs 15:8, the wicked sacrifices are abomination to the Lord but he delights in the prayers of those who do right.

What we ask for in prayer, should not be for selfish reasons because God know the heart.

John 14:14, ask anything in Jesus' name and he will do it.

Matthew 21:22 Jesus said,

> "And all things, whatsoever ye shall ask in prayer, believing ye shall receive it" KJV

Just trust and believe that your prayer will be heard and answered by God.

YES, NO AND WAIT

God always answers prayers with yes, no, or wait:

King David woke up each morning seeking God's presence and finding satisfaction by praying.

King David also prayed so he could communicate with God, spending sweet moments with him; he included in his prayers: God would protect him from his enemies, get directions on how to lead the people of Israel (God's chosen people), help in his time of need, give thanks and praises for what God had done.

The Book of Psalms, in the Old Testament, are prayers and hymns to God written by King David.

Psalm 40:1-17, King David cried out for help from God in the face of his enemies and God heard and answered his prayers by granting his request, meaning **YES.**

God knows every person's heart so he cannot be deceived by anyone, so be mindful when you pray that it lines up with God's word.

James 4:3, do not ask God in prayer with the wrong motives because God knows the true heart of everyone, so if we do not receive in our asking it is because of God knows our motive would be spent on pleasures that are not good for us.

God's answer here is **NO**.

Job was a man of God and was cursed by Satan:

Job 1:1-8, NIV

Satan, went before God along with other angels, God asked Satan "where you come from?" Satan said "From roaming through the earth and going back and forth on it," God said "Have you considered my servant Job?", "Job, there is no one on earth like him, he is blameless and a upright man, and he fears (reverence) God and shuns (avoids) evil."

Satan asked "Does Job fear God for nothing, have you not put a hedge around him and his household and everything he has. You have blessed the work of his hands so that his flocks and herds are spread throughout the land, but now stretch out your hand and strike everything he has, and he will surely curse you to your face." (9-11)

God told Satan "Very well, then, everything he has is in your power, but on the man himself do not lay a finger." (12)

Satan left from God's sight; he caused all of Job's children, livestock, and some of his servants to be killed. At that moment, Job tore his robe and fell down to the ground in worship saying *"naked I came from my mother's womb, and naked I will depart. The Lord gave and the Lord has taken away; may the name of the Lord be praised."* (13-21) NIV

In all Job had lost he did not sin or charge God with any wrongs. (22)

Job 2:1-3, NIV

The second time the angels presented themselves before God and Satan again was with them. God again asked Satan *"where had he come from?" Satan again replied said "From roaming through the earth and going back and forth on it,"* God said *"Have you considered my* servant Job?" God repeated all that he had mentioned about Job adding *"And he still maintains his integrity though you incited me against him to ruin him without any reasons."*

Satan replied *"Skin for skin, a man will give all he has for his own life. But stretch out your hand and strike his flesh and bones, and he will surely curse you to your face."* (4-5)

God said *"You may do whatever you choose to do to Job but you cannot take his life."* (6)

Immediately, Job was afflicted just after losing all his possessions, his children, now covered with sores from the soles of his feet to the crown of his head. (7).

Job's wife wondered why he was holding on to his integrity and said *"curse God and die"* but he still continued to trust in God. (9) NIV

Job told her what she was saying was foolish talk, he mentioned to her if we can accept good things from God then why can't we accept the bad things as well but Job didn't sin against God. (10)

Job's three friends (Eliphaz, Bildab and Zophar) wanted him to confess to them about the sins they thought he had committed against God. (11)

Self-reflection: Job asked a great question if we can accept good things from God why can't we accept the bad things that happen to us.

Job continued to tell his friends that he has done nothing wrong against God, and that he still trusted in God even with all he was going through.

Job was seeking his witness from heaven on his behalf, Job 9:33 and 16:19-20.

We know who in heaven arbitrates for us in the present of God, JESUS!

1st John 2:1,

As children of God, hoping we do not sin, but if we do, seek forgiveness through Jesus Chris; who is our righteousness, he will be an advocate on our behalf with the Father.

Job had to **WAIT**, but he would eventually be restored after interceding for his friends who thought he had sinned against God and he gave Job twice as much of what Job had before, Job 42:8-10.

Job went through every emotion a person could go through; pain, suffering, anguish, grief, calamity, and weakness in his flesh; but he didn't lose faith in God.

Read this again, with all of that he had lost, his friends judging him, Job's wife telling him to die, and all the physical elements he suffered, still, Job continued to believe and trust in God. WOW!!!

Self-reflection: How would you have felt or what would you have done if you were Job? Would you have listened to your friends, your spouse telling you to kill yourself, or would you hold firm to your faith?

We must wait on God, in his time he will answer our prayers.

Romans 8:25, what we hope for will be as we wait patiently with resolution though we have not seen it.

HATE

Hate means loves less or no love and it does not come from God.

Love is more powerful than hate because GOD IS LOVE; 1ˢᵗ John 4:8.

Luke 6:35, love and do well to our enemies, help them without expecting anything in return. Our reward will be greater in heaven, because God is kind to the ungrateful and evildoers.

We may not ever see how our showing love will benefit someone who may have been an enemy, but we know God sees all and can break a hardened heart or open up a mind to be loved.

Psalm 97:10, the Lord preserve the soul of the saints for they love him and hate evil and the Lord delivered them from the devil's hand.

John15:17-19 Jesus says,

> "These things I command you that you love one another.
>
> If the world hates you, you know it hated Me before it hated you.
>
> If you were of the world, the world would love its own, yet because you are not of the world, but I chose you out of the world, therefore the world hates you." NKJV

Self-reflection: to love God you must hate all that is evil just like him, for God delivered us out of the hands of the devil through his son, Jesus Christ.

Proverbs 6:16-19, describes the six things God hates and the seven are detestable to him:

1. proudly eyes
2. lying tongue
3. hands that kill innocent individuals
4. hearts of people whom plan to do evil
5. having intentions to run to do evil
6. witnesses whom speaks lies
7. anyone causing family members to fight

UNDERSTANDING

Understanding is comprehending information that is being conveyed to a listener.

The word of God can be challenging to understand since there are so many interpretations of what is being stated from other people's point of views or religious dialogue.

1st John 4:1, brothers and sisters do not believe every spirit but test the spirit, because there are some that have gone out into the world teaching falsely who consider themselves prophets.

The true way to understand God's word is asking him to bless us with wisdom to gain knowledge and understanding.

God asked Solomon "..........Ask for whatever you want me to give you" 1st Kings 3:5 (NIV).

God was pleased with Solomon request for a discerning heart, wisdom, and he became the wisest man ever on earth; (12), there would never be anyone else wiser like King Solomon.

1st Kings 4:29, King Solomon was given great wisdom and exceedingly great understanding and his heart was so large like the sand on the seashore.

Because he had so much wisdom, he became wiser to lead God's people, the children of Israel.

Psalm 14:1, a foolish person says in their heart there is no God is corrupt, who have evil intentions and these people do no good.

Proverbs 4:7, the principal thing is wisdom, as we gain wisdom we get an understanding.

Proverbs 14:6, a mocker tries to seek wisdom but are unable to find it, but whose who seek after knowledge are able to gain an understanding.

KNOWLEDGE

Knowledge is collecting facts and information to determine the ability of seeking wisdom and gaining understanding.

The saying, **knowledge is power** is true, even in learning the word of God. God will give knowledge, to demonstrate to you that his words and actions he performs are true. **TRUE!**

Proverbs 9:9-10

> "Give instruction to a wise man and he will be still wiser still; teach a just man, and he will increase in learning.
>
> The fear (reverence) of the Lord is the beginning of wisdom: and the knowledge of the Holy One is understanding." NKJV

Proverbs 10:14, knowledge is stored up in wise people but a foolish person speaks destruction.

As mentioned previously foolish people have no good intentions and therefore cannot understand the will God.

1st Timothy 2:4, Paul wanted to tell everyone that he desired all men to be saved and obtain the knowledge of truth.

Proverbs 16:27, an ungodly person that digs up evil, and his lips burn with destruction.

In other words, an idle mind is the devils workshop. We need to keep our minds sharp by reading the word of God; making and taking the time to read about him will increase our knowledge of God and his purpose for our daily living.

2nd Peter 3:18, as we continue our walk with God continue to grow in his grace and knowledge through his son, Jesus Christ to him is the glory now and forever.

WISDOM

Wisdom is based on knowledge, the more we grow with knowledge, and wisdom is gained.

Proverbs 8:14, Solomon mentioned that God gives counsel and sound wisdom; he is understanding and has strength.

James 3:17, wisdom from above is more exceeding pure then tranquility, kindness, submission, compassion, good fruits, without partiality and hypocrisy.

The wisdom that God promotes is peace and understanding not confusion, discourse, or misunderstanding. God gives wisdom to those that seek after him.

Proverbs 1:2-3, 5

> "To know wisdom and instruction, to perceive the words of understanding;
>
> To receive the instruction of wisdom, justice, judgment, and equity;
>
> A wise man will hear and increase learning, and a man of understanding will attain wise counsel." NKJV

Proverbs 1:7, reverence of the Lord is the start of knowledge but fools hate wisdom and instructions.

Proverbs 8: 8-11

> "All the words of my mouth are just; none of them crooked or perverse.
>
> To the discerning all them are right; they are upright to those who have found knowledge.
>
> Choose my instruction instead of silver; knowledge rather than choice gold,
>
> For wisdom is more precious than rubies, and nothing you desire can compare to her." NIV

Combining these three; understanding, knowledge, and wisdom, as God has stated in his own word, these are more precious than metals or gems on this earth.

SUBMISSION

Submission is adhering to something or someone that has authority; we are called to be in submission to God.

James 4:7, we must submit ourselves to God rebuke the devil and he flee from us.

When we are letting God lead our lives we are submitting to him and his way.

Ephesians 5:21, Paul was speaking to the church of Ephesus:

The church needs to submit to God as well as among each other to strengthen and edify the congregation in the reverence of God.

Ephesians 5:22-33, Paul went on to compare the submission to God to the family structure; the husband is the head of the wife and the children, as God is the head of the family.

1st Peter 5:6, we should humble ourselves under the mighty hand of God that he will lift us up in the last days.

Self-reflection: Being able to allow yourself to be submitted under God mighty hand shows humbleness and your willingness to let him guide and lead you.

And if you don't submit to God you are going to submit to something, we all do at some point whether it is an addiction, physical or mental attributes; something is going to put you in submission.

Why not submit yourself to God, and then you will know that you have the creator directing your life and not something that can or will destroy your life.

THE CHURCH

Church is a translation of ekklesia, meaning called out or assembly, the church are a group of baptized believers.

Matthew 16:13-18 Jesus asked his disciples;

"Who do men say that I, the Son of Man, am?"

So they said, *"some say that you are John the Baptist: some Elijah; and others, Jeremiah, or one of the prophets."*

Jesus asked them: *"But who do you say that I am?"*

And Simon Peter answered and said; *"You are the Christ, the Son of the living God."*

And Jesus answered and said unto him, *"Blessed are you, Simon Bar-Jonah for flesh and blood has not revealed this to you but, My Father who is in heaven."*

"And I also say to you that you are Peter, and on this rock I will build My church and the gates of Hades will not prevail against it." NKJV

The church is not the building; it is the collective baptized believers of God inside the building.

Jesus referred back to the Old Testament (Isaiah 56:7) about the temple of God as a house of prayer (Matthew 21:13).

DEATH

Death is the termination or ending of life, it will come to us all.

Ecclesiastes 12:7, from the dust we came and to dust we will return but the spirit will return to God who gave it to us.

Psalms 104: 29, God hides his face from us, we are concerned when God takes our last breath, and we die, then our bodies return to the dust.

Genesis 1:26-27, in the beginning when God created the heavens and the earth, on the sixth day he created man.

From the dust of the earth and breathe life into it, becoming a living soul named, Adam.

From the earth we came and to the earth we shall return, it is only our fleshy body that will return to the earth but our spirit goes back to God.

2nd Corinthians 5:8, to be separated from the body is to be in the presence of the Lord.

When someone dies I don't feel too sad because I know they are back with the Lord. But I also pray they had a relationship with God I desire that no one goes to hell but are waiting to arise from death and spend eternity with the Lord.

Everyone's spirit must return to the Lord, believers and non-believers for judgment in the end of days:

Revelation 20:13, everything on this earth gave up its dead and hell also delivered its dead and the dead was judged according to their works.

Proverbs 14:27, the reverence of the Lord is a fountain of life, so it is able to turn us away from the traps of death.

1st Corinthians 15:55-57, where is death's sting and where is hell's victory? Death's strength comes from sin, but thank God for his begotten son, Jesus Christ, for he has given us the victory over death.

Jesus died for our sins, now we can be forgiven by God for breaking any of the law's we are commanded to follow. Before Jesus's death, sin would have condemned us all to death but again Jesus took our place because of the love, our father has for us.

Romans 6:7-10

"For he who has died has been freed from sin,

Now if we died with Christ, we believe that we shall also live with Him.

Knowing that Christ, having been raised from the dead, dies no more, Death no longer has dominion over Him.

For the death, that He died, He died to sin once for all; but the life that He lives. He lives to God." NKJV

BOOK OF LIFE

Revelation Chapter 20:12-15, there will be two books opened, one contains the names of the dead (non-believers) of all ages and the Book of Life is the names of the baptized believers of God of all ages as well:

Exodus 32:32-33

> *"Yet now, if You will forgive their sin but if not, I pray, blot me out of Your book which You have written.*
>
> *And the Lord said to Moses whoever has sinned against Me, I will blot him out of My book."* NKJV

Psalms 69:27-28, those that work in iniquity will add on to it, and will not be lead to God's righteousness. They will not be in the book of life nor written with those that are righteous.

Daniel 12:1

> *"At that time Michael shall stand up, the great prince who stands watch over the sons of your people, and there shall be a time of trouble, such as never was since there was a nation, even to that time, and at that time your people shall be delivered everyone who is found written in the book."* NKJV

Act 3:19, we need to repent and convert to God, for our sins to be wiped away we may become renewed with the Lord.

The blood of Jesus covers a multitude of sin and when you believe in him, repent, and follow him; your name will be written in the Book of Life.

Matthew 26:28, Jesus' blood is the new covenant which he shed on the cross for us in forgiveness of sins.

1st Peter 4:8, above all things we must have sincere love for one another because Jesus' love, the shedding of his blood covers a multitude of sin.

Matthew 13:24-29

Jesus told a parable of the sower, a man planted good seeds (wheat) in a field and then went to bed, as he was sleeping his enemy came along and planted bad seeds (tares) in the same field with the good seeds.

When the man woke up, his servants questioned him, if he had planted good seeds and he responded with yes, the servants wondered how the tare (bad seeds) got planted. The man told the servants that his enemy planted the tare, the servants wanted to know if they should remove the tare, the man responded with no let them grow together because if you try to pull up the tare you may pull up wheat in the process.

Matthew 13:37-40 Jesus says,

> "He who sows the good seed is the Son of Man.
>
> The field is the world, the good seeds are the sons of the kingdom, but the tares are the sons of the wicked one.

*The enemy who sowed them is the devil, the harvest is
the end of age, and the reapers are the angles.*

*There as the tares are gathered and burned in the fire,
so it will be the end of this age."* NKJV

Revelation 20:15, anyone that is not found in the Book of Life will be
cast into the lake of fire.

SUBSTANCE

Substance is "which stands under Faith", as discussed earlier faith is truly believing and trusting in God.

Substance, enforces the meaning of the realization of what you believe will be without seeing the results and knowing for sure without doubting.

Hebrews 11:1, faith is hoping for the substance of needs we are desiring to see, the proof of the needs not seen.

Substance also represents possessions or material things.

Deuteronomy 33:11, Moses was telling the tribes of the Children of Israel, the Lord would bless their substances and accepts the works their hands and strike those who rise against them, those who hate them, and their enemies would not rise again.

Ezra 9:1-15, Ezra, a priest to the Israelites, was weeping and praying confessing to God for the men's disobedience, because the men were marrying pagan women which God had commanded them not to do.

Ezra 10:8-19, Ezra asked the men to separate themselves from their wives and children or they will forfeit all their substances that God had for them.

DOUBT

Doubt is not having faith to believe that something is true.

Self-reflection: Is it human nature to doubt?

Matthew 14: 21-26

Jesus requested his disciples get in a boat and go before him to the other side of the shore after feeding the five thousand; as Jesus sent the multitude away, he went up to the mountain to pray. As evening came he was alone on the mountain, the boat that the disciples were in was being tossed in the middle of the sea by waves because the winds were fierce.

As the boat continued to be tossed by the winds and waves the disciples saw Jesus walking on the water and became troubled thinking it was a ghost and cried out in fear.

But immediately Jesus spoke to them saying *"Be of Good Cheer! It is I, do not be afraid."*(27)

Peter replied *"Lord if it is you command me to come to You on the water."*(28)

Jesus told Peter to *"Come"*, when Peter step out of the boat on the water to go to Jesus, he saw the wind was boisterous he was afraid and began to sink crying out to him *"Lord, save me."* (29-30)

And immediately Jesus stretched out his hand and caught him up and said to Peter "O *you of little faith, why did you doubt.*" (31) NKJV

Mark 11:11-14,

One morning Jesus and his disciples were walking to Jerusalem and on their way Jesus saw a fig tree with nothing but leaves on it. He spoke to the tree and said "*Let no one eat fruit from you ever again.*" NKJV

The next day Jesus and his disciples left the city as they were walking Peter noticed the fig tree, and remembering what Jesus had said to it, Peter mentioned it to Jesus. (19-21)

Jesus replied:

> "*Have faith in God.* (22)
>
> *For assuredly, I say to you, whoever says to this mountain, Be removed and be cast into the sea, and does not doubt in his heart, but believes that those things he says will be done, he will have whatever he says.* (23)
>
> *Therefore I say to you, whatever things you ask when you pray believe that you receive them, and you will have them.*" (24) NKJV

Acts 2: 6-13

During the time of Pentecost there were people from all over the nations hearing the baptized believers filled with the Holy Spirit speaking in tongues which were not their native languages and the nations whom saw this were in doubt to what they were hearing and seeing. The excuse the nations came up with to justify their reasoning was the baptized believers were full of new wine.

Believers can doubt as well:

John 20:19-24

The disciples were assembled together when they were told Jesus had risen and when Jesus appeared the first time a disciple named Thomas was not with them.

When Thomas was told that Jesus had risen he doubted and mentioned unless he saw Jesus hand prints of the nails and put his finger into the prints, put his hand into Jesus' side he would not believe. (25)

Eight days passed and then Jesus appeared to the disciples, Thomas was among them, Jesus said to Thomas *"Reach your finger here, and look at My hands; and reach your hand here, and put it into My side. Do not be unbelieving but believing."* Then Thomas acknowledged Jesus, but he told Thomas *"because you have seen Me you have believed. Blessed are those who have not seen and yet have believed."* (26-29) NKJV

GOD WORDS ARE TRUE! We must never doubt but always BELIEVE!

Romans 14:23, the people whom doubts are guilty for doubting and not for consuming faith, no matter what, it is not from faith, it is sin.

FAVOR

Favor is having a good standing with God.

The Israelites had favor with God even when they were in captivity from their time in Egypt (Exodus Chapters 1-15), to being captured by the Cushan-Rishathaim, Judges 3:8 and so many other times for their disobedience towards God; which caused the Israelites to be captured by other nations, but God continued to show favor.

Acts 2:14-47

In the time of Pentecost, Peter was speaking to the people and they were becoming saved (repenting, confessing and being baptized), as they were praising God all in one place; God showed favor and the congregation increased daily.

In finding favor with God, we are blessed in the sight of men, women, and everything that we desire according to his promise will come to pass.

Proverbs 12:2, a good person obtains favor from God, but people with wicked intentions are condemned.

PROMISE

Promise is a declaration or assurance of a situation or circumstances that will happen or occur.

The promise that those whom believe in God, Jesus, and the Holy Spirit by confessing our sins and being baptized we will be with them in Heaven for all eternity.

1st John 2:24-25

> "As for you, see that what you have heard from the beginning remains in you. If it does, you also will remain in the Son and in the Father.
>
> And this is what he promised us-eternal life." NIV

God promises never fail.

Joshua 23:14

Joshua was giving his last address to the Israelites on the day he was dying and telling them, all they knew in their hearts and soul God had never failed them. And the good things that God had blessed them had come to pass and again God had never failed them.

Hebrews 6:18

There are two unchangeable things about God, it is impossible for him to **lie**. We should be comforted, for we run towards hope; which is set before us, we should be greatly encouraged.

God's **promise** is the other unchangeable thing mentioned in this scripture.

Promise is also a covenant, as God made a covenant with Noah that he would never again flood the earth with water.

Genesis 9:8-17, as a token of the covenant God placed a rainbow in the sky and every time it is seen it is the promise that God made to the world.

When we become baptized believers of God we are making a promise that we will follow his directions for our lives. We are no longer bound by our own selfish ways but look to God to lead and guide us in our daily lives until we are with him in Heaven.

Exodus 19:5

God was telling the people on earth that we should obey his voice, his covenants and then we will be special treasures to God placing us above all people, for the all earth is His.

CONFESSION

Confessing is admitting before God we are sinners and through Jesus' death, burial, and resurrection; also acknowledging to the world, that we have been saved and have been set apart from it; for we now trust and believe in God Almighty.

Matthew 10:32-33

> "Therefore whoever confesses Me before men, him I will also confess before My Father who is in heaven."

Self-reflection: If you decide not to confess Jesus stated *"But whoever denies Me before men him I will also deny before My Father who is in heaven."* NKJV

1st John 4:15

As we confess that Jesus is the Son of God; God resides in us and we in God.

TEMPTATION

Temptation is a desire or enticement that can cause us faultier into sin against the will of God.

We all have been tempted in some way or another, it may or may not have been beneficial but we did it anyway, whether pressure from family, friends or we convinced ourselves into it.

1st Timothy 6:9, having the desire to be rich, we can fall into temptation or a trap; which can cause many to fall into foolish and harmful lust that we as people can end up in destructive or doomed behavior.

We can put ourselves into temptation, which may lead us into harmful consequences.

But we need to remember, when we put ourselves in the pit of temptation, God has us and will restore us back to him because we cannot do it on our own.

1st Corinthians 10:13

Temptation cannot overwhelmingly overtake us, except what temptation is common to mankind, but we know God is faithful, and will not allow us to be tempted beyond what we are not able to handle and he will make an escape for us to be able to bear through it.

There are temptations that we will encounter on a daily basis while on this earth that can cause us to fall, but God is stronger than any temptation that will try to defeat us.

James 1:2-3

> "My brethren count it all joy when ye fall into divers' temptations.
>
> Knowing this that the trying of your faith worketh patience." KJV

2nd Peter 2:9, the Lord knows how to deliver the godly from temptation and to reserve the unrighteous to the punished in the last days for judgment.

Again, God is always with his children even when we fall into temptation, our faith in him will give us happiness and joy knowing he will not leave us but help guide us through as we are being delivered from temptation.

GUILT

Guilt is admitting doing something wrong towards somebody, or evidence proves that wrong was committed by a person, in God's eye we are all guilty of sin.

If one sin is committed from the law then all have been broken as stated in:

James 2:10,

As we keep the whole laws but fell short on one then all laws were broken.

Romans 3:9-20, NKJV

Shows us that no one is righteous under the law God had given:

> "What then? Are we better than they? Not at all. For we have previously charged both Jews and Greeks that they are all under sin.
>
> As it is written: There in none righteous no not one.
>
> There is none who understands there is none who seeks after God.

They have all turned aside they have together become unprofitable; there is none who does good no not one.

Their throat is an open tomb; with their tongues they have practiced deceit the poison of asps is under their lips.

Whose mouth is full of cursing and bitterness?

Their feet are swift to shed blood;

Destruction and misery are in their ways;

And the ways of peace they have not known

There is no fear of God before their eyes.

Now we know that whatever the law says it says to those who are under the law, that every mouth may be stopped and all the world may become guilty before God.

Therefore by the deeds of the law no flesh will be justified in His sight, for by the law is knowledge of sin." NKJV

The Ten Commandments, statutes, and precepts are God's law given to the Israelites (Deuteronomy 5:6-21, 22-33).

1st John 2:4, if someone says they know God but do not follow after him is a lair and there is no truth in them.

Again, we are all guilty of sin and must repent to be forgiven!!

BEATITUDE'S

Matthew Chapter 5 is the Beatitudes from Jesus' sermon on the mountain, it describes all the blessings one will receive or be rewarded for being obedient to God.

> 3,"*Blessed are the poor in spirit: for theirs is the kingdom of heaven.*"

> 4," *Blessed are those who mourn: for they will be comforted.*"

> 5, "*Blessed are the meek: for they will inherit the earth*"

> 6, "*Blessed are those who hunger and thirst for righteousness: for they will be filled.*"

> 7, "*Blessed are the merciful; for they will be shown mercy.*"

> 8, "*Blessed are the pure in the heart: for they will see God.*"

> 9,"*Blessed are the peacemakers: for they will be called the children of God.*"

> 10, "*Blessed are those who are persecuted because of righteousness, for theirs is the kingdom of heaven.*"

11, "Blessed are you when people insult you, persecute you, and falsely say all kinds of evil against you because of me."

12, "Rejoice and be glad, because great is your reward in heaven, for in the same way they persecuted the prophets who were before you." NIV

The beginning of these verses, "Blessed" means happy; these are characteristic of those that have humbled themselves to the will of God.

These verses give us a balance of the gifts God provides to us inwardly and the promise of the kingdom to come for all we have suffered on this earth for his name sake.

And in verse 12, we are to be exceedingly glad in knowing, with all the persecutions and hatred we may endure while serving God, a great reward awaits us in heaven.

BORN-AGAIN

Those who are born-again, they have turned away from their wicked ways (sin) and accepted God, Knowing evil will not prevail against the kingdom of God.

John 3:3, 5-6 Jesus says:

> "Mostly assuredly, I say to you unless one is born-again he cannot see the kingdom of God"
>
> "Most assuredly I say to you unless one is born of water and the Spirit he cannot enter the kingdom of God.
>
> That which is born of the flesh is flesh and that which is born of the Spirit is spirit." NKJV

Through Jesus Christ we have been redeemed having been baptized physically but also spiritually and we will inherit all God has promised, eternity in heaven.

GOD LONGS FOR US

God is more of a true companion to us then we can be to each other or to ourselves. People can be so two-faced at times but it's so wonderful to know God will never be that way with us; he will never abandon us when we need a friend in times of trouble:

John 15: 13-17

> "Greater love has no one than this than to lay down one's life for his friends.
>
> You are friends if you do whatever I command you
>
> No longer do I will call you servants, for a servant does not know what his master is doing but I have called you friends, for all things that I heard from My Father I have made known you.
>
> You did not choose Me, but I chose you and appointed you that you should go and bear fruit, and that your fruit should remain that whatever you ask Father in My name He may give you.
>
> These things I command you, that you love one another."
> NKJV

Self-reflection: taking the time to speak to God will build a stronger foundation with your relationship with him.

Proverbs 18:24, unreliable friends do us no good but there is a friend that will stick closer to us more than a sibling

Self-reflection: If we can show our friendliness towards others, how is it that we can't acknowledge God? He so desires to be our friend.

God is our main companion though we are not able to physically see him; he is here, he desires us to communicate with him on a daily basis.

Isaiah 41:10, 13

> *"Fear not, for I am with you, be not dismayed for I am your God. I will strengthen you, yes, I will help you; I will uphold you with My righteous right hand.*
>
> *For, I the Lord your God will hold your right hand, Saying to you, Fear not, I will help you."* NKJV

God wants to hear our voices, thoughts, ideas, desires, troubles, and even our complaints, though he already knows it all, he just wants us to acknowledge and recognize him; God is a friend, a true loving friend.

Psalm 119:63, God is a friend to us if we fear him and follow his precepts.

PRECEPTS

Precepts are instructions given from superior authority, regarding the duties required of the ones underneath them.

God is that superior authority and he is requiring us to follow the commandments he has given, the two greatest ones:

Mark 12: 30-31

> "And you shall love the Lord your God with all your heart, with all your soul, with all your mind and with all your strength. This is the first commandment.
>
> And the second like it is this: You shall love your neighbor as yourself. There is no other commandment greater than these." NKJV

Psalm 119:4, God has laid down his precepts; it is to be followed and obeyed to the fullest.

Restating that, we must recognize that God's precepts must be followed and obeyed according to God's will to the best of our abilities.

Following and obeying God, will forever lead us to the blessings he has for us on this earth, as well as being with him in heaven.

The other commandments are just as important as the first two. It is the 10 commandments and the first four are pertaining to God and the last six are pertaining to us toward others.

Exodus 20: 3-17;

1. *"You shall have no other gods before Me"* (3)
2. *"You shall not make for yourself a carved image any likeness of anything that is in heaven above or that is in the earth beneath, or that is in the water under the earth"* (4)
3. *"You shall not take the name of the Lord your God in vain, for the Lord will not hold him guiltless who takes his name in vain"* (7)
4. *"Remember the Sabbath day and to keep it holy"* (8)
5. *"Honor your father and your mother, that your days may be long upon the land which the Lord your God is giving you"* (12)
6. *"You shall not murder"* (13)
7. *"You shall not commit adultery"* (14)
8. *"You shall not steal"* (15)
9. *You shall not bear false witness (lie) against your neighbor"* (16)
10. *"You shall not covet your neighbor's house; you shall not covet your neighbor's wife, or his female servants, or his ox, or his donkey, or anything that is your neighbor's"* (17) NKJV

Psalm 119:15, we should meditate on God's precepts and contemplate on His ways.

This scripture is informing us that we need mediate and examine our lives on the way and will of God.

Self-reflection: Are you living the life that is pleasing in God's sight or can you strive to live a life that would be pleasing in the sight of God.

STATUTES

A statute is a law or decree, God expects us to follow his statutes because his judgments are true, and those whom refuse to follow his statutes are punished.

The statues were prescribed within God's law: the covenants, precepts, and commandments which include his grace and mercy.

How can grace and mercy really be in sync with God's statutes?

Answer: the laws itself is the characteristic of God's grace and mercy, he enables us to worship him for whom he is; being obedient to God's law gives us life.

Psalm 119:5, King David was firmly acknowledging and obeying God's decrees by his words and actions.

Psalm 119:145, King David cried out to God with his whole heart, that he would keep the Lord's statutes.

Ezra 7:8-27, after seeking God's guidance, Ezra was given God's statutes and laws for the Children of Israel when he returned to Jerusalem.

As we are guided by God's statues and laws we are being drawn closer to him.

Psalm 119:16, we should delight ourselves in the God's statutes and not forget his words.

Matthew 5:17, Jesus stated "Do not think that I came to destroy the Law or the Prophets. I did not come to destroy but to fulfill."

These precepts and statues are from the Old Testament though there are debated about these topics about whether or not Jesus fulfilled these laws in the New Testament, however, Jesus stated in Matthew 5:18

".....Till heaven and earth pass away one jot or one tittle will by no means pass from the law till all is fulfilled."

In verse 19, Jesus mentioned that whoever breaks these commandments and teach others to do the same are the considered the least in the kingdom of heaven, however, those who follow the commandments and teaches others to do so are great in the kingdom of heaven.

The shedding of Jesus' blood is a new covenant, which is shed for the remission of our sins. This new covenant is not just through his blood, but also his Word and his Spirit.

SIN

Sin is the one thing that keeps us from God because it is the total opposite of his will.

1st John 3:4, whoever commits sin also breaks the law, for sin is a law breaker; a sinner breaks God's law.

1st John 5:16-17, if we see a brother or sister in Christ sin that does not lead to death pray for them so God can provide them with life. There is sin that leads to death and then there is sin that leads not to death, for all unrighteousness is sin, but there is sin leading not to death.

This scripture tells us that if we sin we can be forgiven, by confessing and sincerely repenting for the sin, but if we intentionally sin and seek not forgiveness it can lead to death, meaning not living eternally in heaven but in hell.

Again to make sure there is an understanding; if we decide to continue sinning and seek not repentance, judgment has been made. But if we choose to turn away from sin and sincerely seek forgiveness from God, then he is just to do so.

1ˢᵗ John 1:9

> "If we confess our sins, He is faithful and just to forgive
> us our sins and to cleanse us from all unrighteousness."
> NKJV

Satan is the mastermind behind sin:

He caused the whole world to sin, and when that occurred, God saw
no one on the earth that could redeem the people back to him, so
Jesus offered up himself as a sacrifice to deliver God's people from sin.

Romans 6:23

> "For the wages of sin is death, but the gift of God is
> eternal in Christ Jesus our Lord." NKJV

John 1:29

John the Baptist was ministering to the people letting them know
that the one, the Lamb of God, who was coming after him would
take away the sins of the world.

Matthew 27:46

When Jesus took upon the sins of this world, the Father could not
look upon him. Before Jesus took his last breath he said "ELI, ELI,
Lama, Sabachthani, "My God, My God why have you forsaken me?"
NKJV

Understanding that we are accountable to God for our sins, we need
to repent and be restored through Jesus Christ then we can truly be
forgiven.

Self-reflection: Our words and actions prove that we are guilty of sinning against God; and he will judge us accordingly. Will you seek repentance or will you face the consequences?

There still will be those that will refuse to listen and not obey God by continuing to do wrong in his sight and not repent, which will cause them not to be blessed by God or live eternally in Heaven.

Isaiah 59:16

> "He saw that there was no man, and wondered that there was no intercessor; Therefore His own arm brought salvation for Him; and His own righteousness, it sustained Him." NKJV

God saw no one on this earth that could redeem us back to him, so Jesus, his son, became the salvation and righteousness as he is now our intercessor, for us to be saved from sin and be redeemed back to God.

Self-reflection: through repentance we can be saved for we were sinners before we came to God, so everyone has the opportunity to be redeemed back to the Father.

Roman 3:23-24

> "For we all have sinned and come short of the glory of God,
>
> Being justified freely by His grace through the redemption of that is in Christ Jesus." NKJV

Romans 6:1-14, we are dead to sin but alive in Christ.

SATAN

Isaiah 14:12-23, Satan was one of the highest angels in heaven and he wanted to be acknowledged above God so he caused a rebellion in heaven.

Satan is described as the originator of sin (1st John 3:8), deceiver (Revelation 12:9), liar and a murder (John 8:44), thief and a destroyer (John 10:10).

Luke 10:18, Satan was expelled from heaven like lighting coming down from the sky.

Because Satan wanted to hurt God, he used God's own creation, man (Human); and try to turn them away from God.

We must not become deceived or foolish; Satan knows how much God loves us, so he tries to deter us from him with temptations and desires that are in our hearts.

The more people he deceives the happier Satan becomes, but we have the means to turn away from sin, and defeat him.

Self-reflection: we do what we want, when we want, and we don't have to be accountable to no one but ourselves, we don't have to be deceived by Satan to think in such a manner because it is our own thoughts and actions of free will.

Remember, Paul stated that there are two natures in us that war with each other on a daily basis: the flesh and the spirit. The flesh desires to do wrong while the spirit desires to do good, Galatians 5:17.

We are held accountable to God whether we are led by our own minds or by Satan.

Genesis 3:1-13,

Satan appeared as a crafty serpent beast; first speaking to Eve questioning God's words about the fruit on the tree of life, he tempted her enough that she ate, then gave to Adam and he ate.

This is called the fall because sin fell upon the earth, Adam and Eve were put out of the Garden of Eden for sinning against God, this was not the only punishment, he made Adam work with his hands, toil for the rest of his days in the fields to grow and provide food for them to eat; Eve was to have pains during child birth and desire her husband who was to lead her. Remember death came upon the earth as previously mentioned in this book.

The serpent got his punishment:

Genesis 3:14-15

> "And the Lord said unto the serpent, because you have done this, you are cursed more than all cattle, and above every beast of the field; on your belly you shall go, and you shall you eat dust all the days of your life.
>
> And I will put enmity (discord or dislike) between you and the woman, and between your seed and her seed;

he shall bruise your head, and you shall bruise his heel."
NKJV

Genesis 4:4-8, this sin allowed for more sin to come upon the earth, Adam and Eve's son Cain killed his brother, Abel, because he was jealous that God accepted Abel's offerings but not his.

DISOBEDIENCE: MOSES AND AARON, AND JONAH

Numbers 20:6, NIV

After Moses lead the children out of Egypt and receiving the ten commandments, the Israelites were complaining there wasn't any water for them to drink, so Moses and Aaron went to the door of the tabernacle and fell on their faces; and glory of the Lord appeared to them;

The Lord spoke to Moses saying, *"Take the staff, and you and your brother Aaron gather the assembly together. Speak to that rock before their eyes, and it will pour out its water. You will bring water out of the rock for the community so they and their livestock can drink."* (7-8)

Moses took the staff before the Lord, as he commanded him. (9)

When Moses and Aaron gathered the Israelites before the rock and said to them, *"Listen you rebels; must we bring you water out of this rock?"* And Moses lifted up his hand and with his staff he struck the rock twice: and the water came out abundantly, and the community drank and their beasts also. (10-11)

Notice, Moses did not speak to the rock; he hit it twice with the staff disobeying God and in doing so;

The Lord said to Moses and Aaron, *"Because you did not trust in me enough to honor me as holy in the sight of the Israelites, you will not bring this community into the land I give them."* (12) NIV

Aaron and Moses both died before the Children of Israel entered into the Promised Land; a promised kept by God, Numbers 20:24-29 and Deuteronomy 34:1-6. Think about that.

Book of Jonah, NIV

1:1-5

Jonah was a prophet of God, he was told by God to go Nineveh and tell the people there that their wickedness had come up before him. But instead Jonah left Joppa to get away from God's order and got on a ship headed to Tar shish, while on the ship there was a great storm. The men aboard the ship cried and feared the horrific storm, but Jonah slept through it.

The captain asked Jonah, *"How can you sleep? Get up and call on your God! Maybe he will take notice of us so that we will not perish."*(6)

Jonah confessed it was his fault that the crew had to deal with the storm that came upon them because he had disobeyed God command by not going to Nineveh. The crew wanted to know what could be done for him, Jonah requested to be thrown overboard and the storm would stop. (7-13)

The crewmen were hesitate to throw him overboard but the storm continued to be fierce, so they threw Jonah into the sea, God had prepared a great fish to swallow Jonah and he was in the belly of the fish for 3 days and 3 nights. (14-17)

Jonah 2:1-10

Jonah prayed to God while in the belly of the fish, crying out about his affliction. Jonah repented and requested forgiveness for his disobedience. God heard Jonah and told the fish to spit him out; Jonah was vomited out of the fish onto dry land.

3:1-4

Jonah then was told a second time to go to Nineveh, Jonah got up and went to the great city. Nineveh was a three day journey from where Jonah had landed, but he made it there in a days' journey.

As I mentioned in the beginning of this book it is better to obey than the alternative.

GOD's WILL, will be DONE!!!!

OBEDIENCE: NOAH AND PETER

Genesis 6:9, 11-12,

Noah found grace in the sight of God, for he was a just and perfect man compared to the men of his generation on the earth. God saw that the earth and man were corrupted and filled with violence.

God expressed to Noah, that the end of all flesh is come before him; all is filled with corruption and with violence, so he must destroy everything that is on the earth. God commanded Noah to build an Ark at his specifications and that every living animal on the earth was to enter the Ark 2 by 2 (male and female) from the smallest crawly thing to greatest of animals (13-22).

Genesis 7:1-24,

Noah obeyed God, he and his family went into the Ark, as it rained for 40 days and 40 nights, destroying every flesh that was not in the Ark.

Simon (Peter) was a fisherman, whose main objective was to catch fish and sale it for profit for income for his family.

Side Note: Peter saw his mother in-law healed from a fever by Jesus, (Matthew 8:14-17, Mark 1:29-31, and Luke 4: 38-39).

Luke 5: 1-3,

A multitude came to hear Jesus preach the word of God as he stood by the lake of Gennesaret, where there were two boats nearby, the fishermen had gone to wash their nets; Jesus entered one of the boats, which happened to be Simon Peter's.

Jesus asked Simon to push the boat a little further off shore, he sat down and taught the multitude, when Jesus had finished teaching; he went and spoke to Simon *"Launch out into the deep; and let down your nets for a catch."* (1) NKJV

Peter informed Jesus that they had toiled all night long, and had nothing to show, however, at Jesus' request, Peter let down the nets. When they had cast out their nets, they gathered a multitude of fish to the point that the nets were beginning to break. (5-6)

Peter and the other fishermen had to call over the other boat to help with the nets; the boats began to sink from the weight of the fishes. When Simon saw it, he fell to his knees telling Jesus to depart from him because he was a sinful man. (7-8)

Jesus said to Simon *"Do not be afraid, from now on you will catch men."* (10) NKJV

Peter objected, at first, but he trusted and obeyed, Peter and the other fishermen were blessed with a bountiful catch of fish; but Peter gained so much more.

Peter became one of the twelve disciples.

When Jesus was arrested Peter denied him 3 times; but he was restored and became an apostle spreading the message of Jesus Christ; Mark 14:72, 16:7 and John 21:1-25.

FAITH: SHADRACH, MESHACH, ABEDNEGO, AND DANIEL

In the Book of Daniel, chapters 1 and 2, Jehoiakim, King of Judah, was put into the hands of Nebuchadnezzar, King of Babylon, and sieged Jerusalem and all that King Jehoiakim ruled because of God.

Children of Israel were put into captivity again:

Daniel 1:1-21, NKJV

Nebuchadnezzar spoke to the master of the eunuch, Ashpenaz, to bring before him certain children of Israel, Jehoiakim's children and his son's children.

These children where well-favored, skilled, and cunning in knowledge, wisdom, understood science, the ability to teach the king to speak and understand Chaldean; the three young men were of royal blood. Their names were Hananiah, Mishael, and Azariah, companions to Daniel, who was a prophet.

King Nebuchadnezzar would feed them daily, his provisions of meat and wine, nourishing them for three years and afterwards they might stand before him.

But they refused to eat the meat and drink the wine because it would defile them; the prince of the eunuchs gave them new names Shadrach, Meshach, and Abednego. The eunuch prince saw favor with Daniel, so he would let them eat vegetarian meals and drink water.

Through God they continued to gain knowledge, skills in all learning and wisdom. When they went before the king, he found that their wisdom and understanding was 10 times better than his magicians and astrologers that where in his entire region.

Daniel 2:1-46

King Nebuchadnezzar had a dream that no one could interpret and became frustrated; when Daniel interpreted his dream the king was so overjoyed he told Daniel, *"Truly your God is a God of gods, and the Lord of Kings, and a revealer of secrets, since you could reveal this secret".* (47) NKJV

The king made Daniel head over the whole province of Babylon, which made him great among other governors over the region, and over the wise men of Babylon. Daniel requested that Shadrach, Meshach, and Abednego be over the affairs of the province of Babylon, (48-49).

Daniel 3:1-7

Now, King Nebuchadnezzar, had an image made out of gold and placed in the plains of Dura, in the province of Babylon, he had sent for the governors, captains, judges, treasures, counselors, sheriffs, and all the rulers come over to the province to have a dedication of the image that the king had set.

When everyone was gathered, they were giving loud praises to the golden image with singing and instruments playing; the gatherers fell down and worshipped the image and those that did not fall down and worship the image were to be immediately put in a burning furnace.

During the time of celebration and worshipping of the image, a certain Chaldean went to King Nebuchadnezzar mentioned to him; that there were certain Jews not honoring his request towards the golden image the king had made, and they oversaw the affairs of the province of Babylon. He went on to tell the king, they do not serve our gods nor worship the image. (7-15)

King Nebuchadnezzar spoke to Shadrach, Meshach, and Abednego, asked them was it true? They answered *"We have no need to answer you in this matter.* (16)

> *"If that is the case our God whom we serve is able to deliver us from the burning fiery furnace, and He will deliver us from your hand, O king."* (17)

> *"But if not, let it be known to you, O king, that we do not serve your gods, nor will we worship the gold image which you have set up."* (18) NKJV

King Nebuchadnezzar, full of rage, commanded that the furnace be heated one seven times more than it was normally heated, he commanded his strongest men to bind the three, and cast them into the fiery furnace with all they had on: coats, hats, pants, shirts, and were cast into it. Because the king's command was so urgent the furnace was so hot that the men who put the three in the furnace were killed by the fire. But the three remained in the furnace; they fell down bound in the midst of the fiery furnace (19-23).

The king was astonished and rose up in haste and began to speak to his counselors asking *".........Did we not cast three men bound into the midst of the fire?"*(24), they replied *"true, O king"*, and then the king said *"Look! I see four men loose, walking in the midst of the fire, and they are not hurt, and the form of the fourth is like the Son of God."*(25) NKJV

King Nebuchadnezzar went near the mouth of the burning furnace and spoke with Shadrach, Meshach, and Abednego asking them; servants of the Most High God come out and come here, Shadrach, Meshach, and Abednego came forward out of the midst of the fire. (26)

Everyone that was gathered with the king saw Shadrach, Meshach, and Abednego come forward from the furnace, their bodies showing no damage from the fire, for it had no power, not a hair of their heads were singed, neither were their clothes changed, nor was the smell of fire upon them. (27)

King Nebuchadnezzar, spoke *"blessed be the God of Shadrach, Meshach, and Abednego, who hath sent his Angel, and delivered his servants who trusted in Him, and they have frustrated the king's word and yielded their bodies, that they should not serve nor worship any god except their own God."*(28) NKJV

The king made a decree that every person, nation, and language, that states anything amiss against the God of Shadrach, Meshach, and Abednego shall be cut in pieces and their houses shall be made of ash heap, because there is no other God that can deliver after this scene. The king promoted Shadrach, Meshach, and Abednego in the province of Babylon (29-30).

Shadrach, Meshach, and Abednego faith did not waiver even in the midst of death, they knew even if they had died God would be with them. That is true encouragement for us that God will always be with us.

Daniel 6:4-10,

Daniel who was mentioned with Shadrach, Meshach, and Abednego, was a president in the province of Babylon, higher than any other president, so the other presidents, princes, governors, counselors, and captains, whom found no fault in Daniel concerning the kingdom nor found any fault in Daniel, himself, so they plotted against Daniel toward the law of his God. These governors and satraps went to King Darius, giving him honor, requested to him to write a firm decree that if any one prays to any God or man and not to him, the king, for 30 days should be cast into the lion's den.

King Darius approved the writing and signed the decree, making it a law that cannot be changed, when Daniel heard this information, he prayed three times a day in his home facing Jerusalem, with his windows opened. (9-10)

Daniel continuously knelt, praying and giving thanks to God as he had done before, and these men, whom had asked for the decree, saw Daniel praying; went to King Darius and told him they saw Daniel praying and they reminded him of the law he had signed and stating it had not changed. That no man gives honor to any God or man within 30 days except for the king, or be cast into the lion's den. The king agreed to their statement, all is true, it was not altered. (10-12)

The plotters also told the king that Daniel who was a captive from Judah, showed no respect to the king because he prays 3 times a day to his God, the king was sorely displeased with himself after hearing about Daniel, and set his heart on delivering Daniel before him. (13-14)

The King Darius pondered on this till the sun went down. The men that plotted against Daniel went back to the king, asked him of the law, it has not changed nor its statute, that the king had established. (11-15)

King Darius commanded Daniel to be brought before him and cast into the lion's den. The king said to Daniel *"Your God whom you serve continually, He will deliver you."* (16) A stone was brought and laid upon the mouth of the den: and the king sealed it with his signet and the signets of his lords, that with these signets nothing changes concerning Daniel (17).

King Darius went home pass the night fasting, no musicians played for him, and he wasn't able to sleep, (18)

King Darius rose very early in the morning and hasted to the lion's den, (19)

When he got to the den he cried with a pained voice unto Daniel saying, *"O Daniel, servant of the living God, has your God, whom you serve continually, been able to deliver you from the lions."* (20) NKJV

Daniel replied to the king;

> *"O king, live forever,*
>
> *My God sent his angel and shut the lion's mouths, so that they have not hurt me. Because I was found innocent before Him; and also, O king, I have done no wrong before you."* (21-22) NKJV

King Darius was exceeding happy for him, and commanded they take Daniel out of the lion's den, so he was taken from the den, there was no harm or hurt to him, because his God delivered him. The king commanded the ones that had spoken against Daniel, to be cast into the lion's den along with their families, so before their bodies could hit the bottom of the den, the lions devoured them all. (23-24)

Again, having faith and trusting in God, we are delivered from our enemies and exalted among those who try to do us harm.

Isaiah 54:17

> *"No weapon forged against you will prevail, and you will refute every tongue that accuses you. This is the heritage of the servants of the Lord, and this is their vindication from me, declares the Lord."* NIV

WOMEN'S ROLE IN MINISTRY AND IN THE HOME

1ˢᵗ Corinthians 14:33-34 and 39-40,

Authorization of confusion does not come from God, for he is the author of peace, this should be instilled in all the saints that consider themselves part of the "church".

The women were speaking in tongues and interrupting the services at the House of God in Corinth. In Paul's letter to the church in Corinth he mentioned the women were doing a disservice to the House God.

1ˢᵗ Corinthians 11:5, 10, 15, Paul understood that women could pray and prophesy in the House of God as long as their heads were covered, but if a woman's head was uncovered it showed dishonor. A woman with long hair is glorified, because the long hair is her covering.

Paul said for "...... women keep silent....." 1ˢᵗ Corinthians 14:34, KJV.

Paul was stating in 1ˢᵗCorinthians 14:35, the wives should ask their husbands questions at home in private and not in public of the congregation because it was deplorable to do so.

Paul, asked the congregation of Corinth to do certain things to get back on track to their main objectives, which are:

1. Remember that Jesus is the foundation of the ministry, 1st Corinthians 4:11.
2. They must do the work of the ministry as one body in Christ Jesus, 1st Corinthians 12:12-26.
3. And love one another, 1st Corinthians 13:4-8.

Self-reflection: you can't bring anyone to God through Jesus Christ when there is conflict within the House of God.

Titus 2:3-5, Paul wrote a letter to Titus telling him to say to the older women, they were to teach the young married women to love their husbands and children. Teaching them how to be homemakers, be obedient to her husband, and do not blaspheme the word of God.

Paul's letter to the Corinthians also included, women that are unmarried, their priority should be about the things of Lord, being holy in both body and spirit. As for the wife, she cares or has concerns about the things of the world in how she should please her husband, 1st Corinthians 7:34.

DEBORAH

Deborah is one of many women in the Bible whom was used by God for his purpose.

Judges 4,

The children of Israel were again doing evil thing in the sight of God, so he had them put into captivity, by the hands of Jabin, King of Canaan. (1-2)

The children of Israel cried out to God; for King Jabin had nine hundred chariots of iron, and for twenty years he had harshly oppressed them. (3)

Deborah was a prophetess, the wife of Lapidoth and a judge for Israel. She held court under the Palm of Deborah, between Ramah and Bethel in the hill country of Ephraim; the Israelites would go to her to have their disputes settled. (4-5)

Deborah sent for Barak, son of Abinoam, she told him:

> "Has not the Lord God of Israel commanded, go
> and deploy troops at Mount Tabor take with you ten
> thousand men of the sons of Naphtali and of the sons
> of Zebulun.

And against you I will deploy Sisera the commander of Jabin's army, with chariots and his multitude at the River Kishon and I will deliver him into your hand?" (6-7) NKJV

Barak replied *"If you will go; but if you will not go with me, I will not go."* (8)

Deborah agreed to go with him, only because of how Barak answered her, she knew the honor belonged to the Lord and not to him, so Deborah went with Barak just as the Lord had requested, they gathered the ten thousand men from Naphatali and Zebulun.

When Sisera was told that Barak had gone to the Mount of Tabor, he gathered together nine hundred iron chariots all the men with him from Harosheth Haggoyim to the Kishon River (9-13).

Deborah spoke to Barak *"Up! For this is the day in which the Lord has delivered Sisera into your hand. Has not the Lord gone out before you?"* So Barak went own Mount Tabor, followed by ten thousand men, at Barak advancement the Lord routed Sisera, all his chariots, and army by the sword. Sisera abandoned his chariots and fled on foot. (14) NKJV

But Barak went after the chariots and the army as far as Harosheth Haggoyim. All the troops of Sisera fell by the sword and were killed, Sisera, however, still fleeing on foot, saw the tent of Jael, the wife of Heber the Kenite, whom had his tent set under a great tree in Zaanannim near Kedesh, Sisera thinking that the relationship was well between the King of Hazor and the clan of the Kenites he went to the tent. (15-17)

Jael went out to meet him and said, *"Turn aside my lord turn aside to me; do not fear."* (18) NKJV

So Sisera went into the tent with Jael, putting a cover over him. Sisera requested a drink of water, for he was thirsty; Jael opened a skin of milk, gave him a drink, and covered him up again. (19)

Sisera requested that Jael stand in the doorway of the tent, so if someone asked *"if there any man here"* that would happen to come by, you could tell them no. (20) NKJV

But Jael instead picked up a tent peg and a hammer, went quietly to him while he lay fast asleep, from exhaustion; she drove the peg through his temple into the ground, and he died. (21)

Barak came by, in the pursuit of Sisera, and Jael went to meet him, She said *"Come, I will show you the man whom you seek."* So Barak went into the tent and saw Sisera, lying dead with a tent peg in his temple, dead. (22) NKJV

On that day God subdued Jabin, the Canaanite king, before the Israelites. And the hand of the Israelites grew stronger and stronger against Jabin, the Canaanite king, until they destroyed him. (23-24)

Just look at God, Won't he do it? YES he will; Deborah obeyed and the children of Israel's enemies were killed.

Trusting and believing in God is the best thing for us as baptized believers. Though the Israelites kept disobeying God, he never left them, even when they were put in captivities so many times for so many years.

God never left the children of Israel; he will never leave us for he is with us today and forever!!

HANNAH

Hannah prayed for many years for a child, as time passed, still no child, but she never lost faith.

1ˢᵗ Samuel 1:5-6,

Hannah, the wife of Elkanah, was barren, but she prayed to God continually that one day she could conceive a child, but year after year, no child was conceived.

Now Elkanah's other wife, Peninnah, would provoke and irritate Hannah when she would go to the temple of Lord, because she couldn't conceive; which caused Hannah to weep and not eat. (7)

Elkanah, her husband would ask her *"why do you weep? Why do you not eat? And why is your heart grieved? Am I not better to you than ten sons? (8) NKJV*

One day after Elkanah, Peninnah and Hannah, had eaten and drank in Shiloh; Hannah got up and went into the tabernacle of the Lord. There Eli, the priest, was sitting on a chair by the doorpost of the Lord's tabernacle, Hannah prayed to the Lord and wept in pain as if there was a bitterness in her soul. (9-10)

She made a vow saying *"O Lord of hosts, if You will indeed look on the affliction of Your maidservant and remember me and not forget Your maidservant but will give Your maidservant a male child, then I will give him to the Lord all the days of his life, and no razor shall come upon his head."* (11) NKJV

As Hannah continued to pray to the Lord, Eli observed her mouth, she was praying from her heart, her lips were moving but her voice was not heard. (12-13)

Eli thought that Hannah was drunk and asked her *"How long will you be drunk? Put your wine away from you."*(14) NKJV

Hannah said *"No my lord, I am a woman of sorrowful spirit. I have drunk neither wine nor intoxicating drink, but have poured out my soul before the Lord,* (15)

> *Do not consider your maidservant a wicked woman for out of the abundance of my complaint and grief I have spoken until now. "* (16)

Eli replied *"Go in peace, and the God of Israel grant your petition which you have asked of Him."* Hannah said *"Let your maidservant find favor in your sight."* Then she went her way and ate something, and her face was no longer down casted. (17-18)

Early the next morning, Hannah, her husband, and the other wife, arose and worshipped before the Lord; then they went back to their home in Ramah. Elkanah had relations with Hannah, and the Lord remembered her, so in the course of time Hannah conceived and gave birth to a son, whom she named Samuel, saying *"Because I have asked for him from the Lord."*(19-20) NKJV

Hannah waited until Samuel was weaned to take him to the temple of the Lord, and he would live there always. Elkanah told Hannah *"Do what seems best to you."* After Samuel was weaned she took the boy with her, who was around 2 or 3 years old, a three year old bull, an ephah of flour, a skin of wine, and she took him into the house of the Lord of Shiloh. (21-24)

When they had killed the bull, they brought the boy, Samuel to Eli. Hannah said to Eli, "O *my Lord As your soul lives, my lord, I am the woman who stood by here, praying to the Lord. For this child I prayed, and the Lord has granted me my petition which I asked for Him. Therefore I also have lent him to the Lord; as long as he lives he shall be lent to the Lord.*" Hannah and Eli worshiped the Lord right there. (25-28) NKJV

Hannah had been barren for many years; weeping and unable to eat, some people could even consider that God did not hear her cries, but he did, and through it all she still had faith.

Self-reflection: if she didn't have faith, why go the temple on a regular basis, because she had to, tradition, or any other reason a person may justify her going.

But the fact she knew in her heart one day she would be blessed and that her son would be a blessing by giving him back to God.

Hannah was sincere in her asking and even more sincere in her vow, she said she would give him back to God when he granted her a son.

Self-reflection: could we make such a vow?

Remember God always answers prayers, but in his time not ours.

An Ephah of flour is equivalent to a bushel or 41.05 pounds of flour.

Hannah's son, Samuel, became a great prophet of the Lord, interceded and instructed the children Israel to follow God, 1st Samuel 7:3-6.

The Israelites went to him when they asked for king, 1ˢᵗ Samuel 8:4-22.

Saul became that king, 1ˢᵗ Samuel 9:17.

God lead Samuel to anoint a young boy that was a Shepard who became the next King, David. 1ˢᵗ Samuel 16:1-13.

BALAAM'S DONKEY

God can use the animals too because he also created them:

Number 22:5,

A man named Balaam from around the area of Pethor. He was summoned from his home land by King Balak, the ruler of Moab, at that time, wanted the Israelites out the land, after they had just left Egypt and settled in area next to him, and Balak wanted Balaam to get them out.

King Balak thought that Balaam could put a curse on the Israelites because they were too powerful for him and that if Balaam could defeat them he could drive the Israelites out of the country. King Balak knew that those who are blessed are blessed, and those who are cursed are cursed (6).

The elders went to Balaam and told him what the king wanted done to the Israelites, Balaam told the elders to spend the night and he will give them the answer when God revealed it to him, so they stayed the night (7-8).

God came to Balaam and asked *"Who are these men with you?"* (9) He answered saying *"Balak son of Zippor, king of Moab, has sent to me saying, look, a people has come out of Egypt and they cover the face of the earth, come now curse them for me, perhaps I shall be able to overpower them and drive them out."* (10-11) NKJV

But God said to Balaam, *"You shall not go with them, you shall not curse the people, because for they are blessed."* (12)

The next morning Balaam got up and said to the Elders, *"Go back to your land for the Lord has refused to give me permission to go with you."*(13), so they returned to the king saying to him, *"Balaam refused to come with us."*(14)

Then Balak sent other princes, more numerous and more distinguished than the first, and they went to Balaam. (15).

They told Balaam *"Please let nothing hinder you from coming to me for I will certainly honor you greatly and I will do whatever you say to me, therefore, please come curse this people for me."*(16-17)

Balaam answered them *saying "Though Balak were to give me his house full of silver and gold I could not go beyond the word of the Lord my God to do less or more.*

Now therefore please you also stay here tonight, that I may know what more the Lord will say to me."(18-19) NKJV

That night God came to Balaam and said *"If the men come to call you, rise and go with them, but only the word which I speak to you that you shall do."*(20) NKJV

Balaam got up in the morning, and saddled his donkey, and went with the princes of Moab, but God was very angry when he went, and the angel of the Lord stood in the road and his sword opposing him. Balaam was riding his donkey, and his two servants were with him. When the donkey saw the angel of the Lord standing in the road with a drawn sword in his hand, she turned off the road into a field; Balaam beat the donkey to get her back on the road. (21-23)

Then the angel of the Lord stood in a narrow path between two vineyards, with walls on both sides. When the donkey saw the angel of the Lord, she pressed close to the wall crushing Balaam's foot against it. So he beat her again.

Then the angel of the Lord moved on ahead and stood in a narrow place where there was no room to turn, to the right or the left. When the donkey saw angel of the Lord, she laid down under Balaam, and he was angry, and beat her with his staff (24-27).

Then the Lord opened the donkey's mouth and said to Balaam, *"What I have done to you that you have struck me these three times."*(28)

Balaam answered the donkey, *"Because you have abused me, I wish there were a sword in my hand for now I would kill you."*(29)

The donkey said to Balaam *"Am I not your donkey on which you have ridden ever since I became yours, to this day? Was I ever disposed to do this to you?"* Balaam replied *"No"*. (30) NKJV

Then the Lord opened Balaam eyes and he saw the angel of the Lord standing in the road with his sword drawn, so he bowed low and fell down on his face. (31)

The angel of the Lord asked Balaam *"Why have you struck your donkey these three times? Behold, I have come out to stand against you because your way is perverse before me.*

> *The donkey saw me and turned aside from me these three times, if she had not turned aside from me, surely I would also have killed you by now and let her live."* (32-33)

Balaam said to the angel of the Lord, *"I have sinned; for I did not know you stood in the way against me. Now therefore if it displeases You, I will turn back."*(34)

The angel of the Lord said to Balaam *"Go with the men, but only the word that I speak to you that you shall speak."* So Balaam went with the princes of Balak (35). NKJV

God is able to use anyone or anything because he created all, and his will; once again GOD's WILL BE DONE!

LORD'S PRAYER

Everyone should know the prayer Jesus prayed, known as the Lord's Prayer,

As, Jesus continued his Sermon on the Mountain, he taught the listeners on how to pray to God;

Mathew 6:

>9. *"Our Father which are in heaven, Hallowed be thee name thy name."*

>10. *"Thy kingdom come Thy will be done on earth as it is in heaven,"*

>11. *"Give us this day our daily bread."*

>12. *"And forgive us our debts, as we forgive our debtors."*

>13. *"And lead us not into temptation but deliver us from evil:*

>*For thine is the kingdom, and the power, and the glory, For-ever, Amen".* KJV

This prayer can be a format to use as a guide when praying to God, by first giving him honor and reverence for who is he and where he reigns. Whatever God performs in heaven we are asking he does the same on the earth.

Asking for God to give us our daily substance, is the same way the animals on this earth are not worried about where there meal is coming from, or how flowers and tree are going to cover themselves in the spring. God is able to provide all the substance we need, Luke 12:22-28. We need not struggle to find all that God is able to provide but trust and believe he will bless us with all we need for we are his children, 29-31.

Philippians 4:19

> "And my God will supply all your needs according to His riches in glory by Christ Jesus." NKJV

Forgiving our debts or trespasses is our sins that we commit, whether knowing or unknowing towards others. We also intercede for those who have wronged us and not hold grudges for the trespass or debt that others have done towards us.

Requesting God to guide us, that we may not be tempted by the evil ways of sin.

Praise him for answered prayer, once again for acknowledging God's kingdom, his authority and the significant of his authority for an eternal manner. We should end our prayer in *Jesus name Amen*, because only through him will our prayers reach the Father.

John 14:6, Jesus said,

> "I am the way, truth and the life. No one comes to the Father except through me." NKJV

John 16:17

> *"You did not choose Me, but I chose you and appointed you that you should go and bear fruit, and that your fruit should remain that whatever you ask Father in My name He may give you."* NKJV

Ending a prayer in *Jesus name, Amen* is the seal for God to receive the prayer, acknowledging that through Jesus Christ who is our mediator, intercessor, and our advocate; we can't get to God except through him.

Self-reflection: think of our prayers as being letters sent through the mail, it will not reach its destination without a stamp. Jesus is our stamp!

JABEZ'S PRAYER

Many years ago, there were a lot books written about the Jabez's prayer:

There are two Chronicles books in the Holy Bible, the first Chronicles chronologically names the generations of the 12 tribes of Israel (Jacob's sons) in chapters 1 and 2.

The Jabez's prayer is the only prayer written in either book. God must have wanted Jabez to be set apart from the other individuals listed in the Chronicles. For what purpose I do not know, but the prayer is another model we can follow because as we read it we can tell Jabez is sincere.

1st Chronicles 4:9-10

Jabez was more honorable than his brothers; His mother had named him Jabez, saying *"Because I bore him in pain."* (9)

Jabez cried out to God of Israel, *"Oh that you would bless me indeed and enlarge my territory, that Your hand would be with me, and that You would keep me from evil, that I may not cause pain."* And God granted his request. (10) NKJV

You can read that, Jabez's prayer is sincere and thoughtful in the request he asked from God. He cried out to God, opened up his heart and boldly made his request known.

Jabez asked God to bless him indeed and enlarge his territory, meaning he wanted blessings that was more than just physical or material. Jabez knew who God was and what he was capable of doing. Jabez requested God to guide his footsteps on his travels and journeys so that he would be blessed and be a blessing towards others not just in his inner circles but more outwardly, whomever he encountered they would be blessed.

Jabez knew God is all powerful and his hands exceeds beyond all human imagination, so requesting guidance from the only one who could lead, guide and shelter him was the reason Jabez asked that of God, not just for himself but for everyone he encountered that he didn't cause harm and that evil wouldn't come against him.

God granted Jabez's request, as we can see that God saw the consecrated heart of Jabez's and he desired to bless him. God can be the same way to us, if we ask in a sincere manner he will grant us our request.

Self-reflection: Jabez wanted everything his hands touched be that of God, if we are mindful that God's hand are our hands would we do anything that could defile him.

The Lord's Prayer and the Prayer of Jabez are awesome prayers that we can use as a cornerstone on a daily basis to give honor, and reverence to God in requesting anything from him that lines up with his will.

CONSECRATED BODY

Consecrated body is a spiritual body (inner spirit) not the flesh body (outward man) that has been broken spiritually to the will of God. The body in this manner is in the same way Jesus broke his body to save us from sin. Our consecrated body is no longer our own, we have given it up as a living sacrifice to the Lord.

God can now use us because he has set us apart from doing evil in his sight to be useful for his purpose.

Roman 12:1-2

> *"Therefore, I urge you, brothers and sisters, in view of God's mercy, to offer your bodies as a living sacrifice holy and pleasing to God this is your true and proper worship.*
>
> *Do not conform to the pattern of this world, but be transformed by the renewing of your mind. Then you will be able to test and approve what God's will is his good, pleasing and perfect will."* NIV

GIVER

A giver is someone with a willing heart to offer things to others such as money, time or to provide service to someone in need. Being a giver is such a godly attribute that those receiving the blessing from a giver may encourage the recipient to do the same.

Being a giver is a serious experience not to be taken lightly because God loves those who give.

2nd Corinthians 9:7

We all should give from our hearts without having a grudge or out of necessity; for God loves us for giving cheerfully.

Matthew 6:1-4

> *"Take heed that you do not do your charitable deeds before men, to be seen by them. Otherwise you have no reward from your Father in heaven.*
>
> *Therefore, when you do a charitable deed, do not sound a trumpet before you as the hypocrites do in the synagogues and in the streets that they may have glory from men. Assuredly, I say to you they have their reward.*

But when you do a charitable deed do not let your left hand know what your right hand is doing,

That your charitable deed may be in secret and your Father who sees in secret will Himself reward you openly." NKJV

A giver does not boast or brag when helping or being charitable to others they do it for the joy of giving.

TITHING

Tithing in the Old Testament was being obedient in giving a tenth of monetary funds or first fruits of the season to God. Tithe means tenth in the Hebrew language.

Some House of prayers asks for tithes along with an offering, the difference between these two giving's is that tithe is a sit amount, a tenth of one's earnings, while an offering can be any amount we want to give.

Leviticus 27:30, tithing is like planting seeds in the ground or fruits produce from trees, for all is the Lord's and it is holy to the Lord.

Malachi 3:8

God even asked *"Will a man rob God? Yet you have robbed me. But you say; In what way have we robbed YOU? in tithes and offerings?"* NKJV

Malachi 3:10

God also said *"Bring all the tithes into the storehouse, that there may be food in My house, and try Me now in this, says the Lord of hosts, if I will not open for you the windows of heaven and pour out for you such blessing, that there will not be room enough to receive it"* NKJV

We know God blesses us in our asking; if it lines up with his will, then we should be able to give back to him.

Proverbs 3:9, reverence God with our wealth, tithing should be presented like the crops of the first fruit of its season.

Tithing now a days is considered to be accordance to the Old Testament teaching not relevant to today, but again, some Houses of Prayer still require tithing.

FASTING

Fasting is refraining or abstaining from substance (food or drink) for a period of time, usually a religious observance.

In the Old Testament the children of Israel would fast when told to by kings, prophets, or as a congregation when crisis arose:

2nd Chronicles 20: 1-3,

When King Jehoshaphat of Judah was told that there was a great multitude coming against them, he feared and sought after the Lord he proclaimed all of Judah to fast.

Ezra 8:21-23,

Ezra the priest concerning Judah and Jerusalem, proclaimed a fasting, submit in order to seek God's protection for themselves, their children, and their substance.

Ezra 10:6,

Ezra also fasted for the sins for the men of Israel for marrying pagan women and having children with them, these men had disobeyed God by marrying pagan women.

Judges 20:26-48,

The children of Israel had been defeated in battle against Gibeah, all went to the House of God, wept and sat there before the Lord and fasted the day until the evening providing up burnt offerings, peace offerings, before the Lord asking him to help them defeat the children of Benjamin and God would deliver the children of Benjamin into their hands.

A person can individually fast in requesting a response from God.

Matthew 17:20-21,

Jesus was telling his disciples that if you believe and not doubt, anything would be possible for them, but this type of faith does not go out without prayer and fasting.

UNBELIEVER

An unbeliever is a person who does not believe or refuses to believe in God.

We, people of God, are called to persuade and compel unbelievers to come to God because we do not want anyone to miss the opportunity for salvation and eternal life. We however, will not push, pull, force, or use scare tactics to convert a unbeliever, we can only give a testimony, a word, a prayer, the rest is up to them whether they will choose to follow God or not.

1st Corinthian 7:12-15

Paul stated that he was speaking these words and not on behalf of the Lord:

If someone decides to marry an unbeliever and they choose to stay in the marriage the unbeliever is sanctified by the believer, however, if the unbeliever decides to depart let them go, God wants his children to live in peace.

We are asked again to be set apart from unbelievers as Paul said to the church in Corinth:

2nd Corinthians 6:14-18

> *"Do not be yoked together with unbelievers, for what do righteousness and wickedness have in common? Or what fellowship can light have with darkness?*
>
> *What harmony is there between Christ and Belial (Satan)? Or what does a believer have in common with an unbeliever?*
>
> *What agreement is there between the temple of God and idols? For we are the temple of the living God," As God has said "I will live with them and walk among them, and I will be their God, and they will be my people."*
>
> *"Therefore come out from them and be separate, says the Lord, touch no unclean thing and I will receive you.*
>
> *I will be a Father to you, and you will be my sons and daughters, say the Lord almighty."* NIV

Self-reflection: John 3:18, we who believe in God are not doomed but for those who don't have already been doomed, because they do not believe Jesus is God's begotten Son.

John 5:38, if we do not have the word of God residing in us then we do not believe in him whom sent Jesus.

John 8:24, for those who choose not to believe in Jesus Christ will die in their sins.

2nd Corinthians 4:4, Satan, the god of this world, has blinded the minds some people on this earth; they have become unbelievers and are unable to see the light of the living God through the gospel of Jesus Christ, the image of God.

Hebrews 3:12, we must be mindful of who we interact with, because unbelievers or the ones that choose do evil, can cause us to stray away from God.

Self-reflection: being an unbeliever doesn't seem to be beneficial, right? We need to recognize that there is someone who is above all things, God, and that his son, Jesus, came to his earth to redeem us back to him because we may have lost our way through sin, or will we have decided that being an unbeliever is better than believing.

WHAT DEFILES US

I previously mentioned the fruits of the Spirit that come from God, here are things that defiles us and separates us from God. These are within the hearts of all mankind;

Mark 7:20-23

Evil thoughts, adulteries, fornications, murders, thefts, covetousness, wickedness, deceit, lasciviousness, an evil eye, blasphemy, pride, and foolishness all these things defile a man from within.

We all know what these defilements are and how they can do harm to us physically, mentally, and spiritually that is why we must hold on to God's fruits of the Spirit to keep us from being destroyed by Satan or we destroying ourselves.

Matthew 12:31-32 Jesus said,

"Therefore I say to you, every sin and blasphemy will be forgiven men, but the blasphemy against the Spirit will not be forgiven men.

Anyone who speaks a word against the Son of Man it will be forgiven him but whoever speaks against the Holy Spirit, it will not be forgiven him, either in this age or in the age to come" NKJV

These scriptures gives the description of an unforgivable or an unpardoned sin.

If a person does not accept or believe their sin is forgiven by the Holy Spirit is denying that God has freed them from their sin.

While we know the Holy Spirit will say "we are forgiven" Satan will say "we are condemned".

We can't listen to Satan whom tries to deceive us to not trust in God and what he said he will do, confess your sins to God and he will forgive us.

SABBATH

The Sabbath day is Saturdays, God created the world in six days on the seventh day he rested. He blessed and sanctified the Sabbath, because it was the day he rested after all he had created; Genesis 2:2-3.

Exodus 31:17,

> "It is a sign between Me and the children of Israel forever, for in six days the Lord made the heavens and the earth, and on the seventh day He rested and was refreshed." NKJV

Exodus 34:21

God told Moses to tell the children of Israel to work for six days and on the seventh day which is the Sabbath, day of rest, even during seasons of planting and harvesting time you must rest.

The Pharisees questioned Jesus why his disciples plucked ears of corn on the Sabbath knowing that it is not lawful:

Mark 2: 25-28

Jesus replied to them saying

"Have you never read what David did when he was in need, and hungry, he and those with him?

How he went into the house of God in the days of Abiathar the high priest, and ate the show bread, which is not lawful to eat except for the priests, and also gave some to those who were with him? NKJV

Mark 2:27-28 Jesus said

"The Sabbath was made for man, and not man for the Sabbath.

Therefore the Son of man is also Lord of the Sabbath." NKJV

Matthew 12:12, Jesus said,

"Of how much more value then is a man than a sheep? Therefore it is lawful to do good on the Sabbath." NKJV

SODOM AND GOMORRAH

2020 was the year of the coronavirus and everyone was afraid of the collapse of the economy, many so many people lost their lives, and others lost their jobs, but only a few acknowledged that God shut everything down.

2nd Chronicles 7:13-14

God told Solomon:

> *"When I shut up heaven and there is no rain, or command the locusts to devour the land or pestilence among My people;*
>
> *If My people who are called by My name will humble themselves and pray and seek My face and turn from their wicked ways then I will hear from heaven and will forgive their sin and heal their land."* NKJV

Reflection: wonder if this world has become like Sodom and Gomorrah, the cities that God destroyed because of their perverse and evil nature, the people no longer acknowledged God in any form.

Genesis 18:23

When God told Abraham his plan for Sodom and Gomorrah, He asked God, "*Wilt thou also destroy the righteous with the wicked?*" KJV

Abraham gave God scenarios; could Sodom be saved if 50 righteous people were living in the city, continuing to numbering it down to 10, (24-32) God answered him saying "*For the sake of ten I, will not destroy it.*" (32)

Genesis 19:1-2

Lot, Abraham's nephew, lived in Sodom and met two men (God's angels) while he was sitting at entrance into the city and requested they stay spend the night with him and leave in the morning.

No, they responded and stated that they would be spending the night in the square. But Lot strongly insisted that they spend the night in his home, and they did; Lot feed them as they got ready for bed, then some men (young and old) surrounded Lot's house outside. (2-4)

The men wanted the two men that were in Lot's house, so they could have relations with them. Lot went outside to speak to the men and told them don't do this wicked thing and offered his two daughters to the men, whom were virgins, but as for these men they were protected under Lot's roof. (5-8)

The men refused Lot's offer and were getting angry because Lot's guests were not coming out of the house and they started putting pressure towards Lot, they started forcing their way in but the guests inside the house reached out and grab Lot; closed the door behind him.

The angles struck the men whom were trying to force their way into the house with blindness so they could not find the door. (9-11)

Then two men, the angels, asked Lot where there anyone else in the city that belonged to his family, because they were going to destroy the city, the outcry to the Lord is so great that he has sent us to destroy it. (12-13)

So Lot went to his sons-in-laws, who pledged to marry his daughters, He told them to hurry and get out of the city, because God is about to destroy it. But the sons-in-law thought Lot was joking, as dawn was approaching, the angels told Lot to get his wife, his daughters out now, or they would be swept away when the city is punished. (14-15)

The men grabbed Lot's hand, his wife hands, and the daughter's hands, and led them safely out the city, for the Lord was merciful to them. (16)

As Lot and his family were hastened out of the city of Sodom, one the angels told them to flee for their lives and do not look back, head toward the mountains not the plains or they will be swept away. Lot requested the angels let them to flee to a town called Zoar, because he was unable to make it to the mountains and he would die. (17-19)

The angels accepted his request and spared Zoar from being overthrown, but told Lot and his family to haste, the angel also told Lot that he could not do anything until they reached the city. When the sun had risen, Lot and his family had reached Zoar, the Lord God rained down burning sulfur on Sodom and Gomorrah out of the heavens. God overthrew those cities and everything that resided in it, including all the living things and the vegetation. Lot's wife turned back to look at the destruction and became a pillar of salt. (20-26)

Afterward, Lot went back to the remains of the cities and remembered that his uncle, Abraham, had saved him from the destruction in the city where he once lived. (27-28)

God showed favor to Abraham, that favor extended to Lot and his family.

This is the first time in the bible that God destroyed cities, but remember this is not the only time he destroyed a wicked nation, in Genesis Chapter 6 and 7 God destroyed the whole earth with water.

GOD KEEP HIS PROMISES

The Father of all creation made a promise to the earth and the living things that dwell upon it; to never flood the world again and a sign to keep that promise was and is the rainbow (Genesis 9:9-17).

Self-reflection: How wonderful it is to know, that God keeps his promises, **but what if God was like us, not keeping promises,** hmmmmm.

There have been plenty of promises that God has kept, just a few were mentioned in the **Promise** topic, but the one we are patiently waiting for is the return of Jesus Christ, so we can spend eternity in the presence of God or eternity in hell which would be very sad for those whom have made that choice.

We also know, even though God's promise not to the flood the earth ever again, but it will be fire that destroys the earth next time.

Malachi 4: 1

> *"For behold the day is coming, burning like an oven, and all the proud, yes, all who do wickedly will be stubble, and the day which is coming shall be burn them up. Says the Lord of hosts that will leave them; neither root nor branch." NKJV*

Stubble is part of a plant stem left standing in the field after the crop has been harvested.

Self-reflection: those that may deny or do not believe, has there been anything in his word (The Holy Bible) that did not come to fruition when God spoke.

LORD'S SUPPER

Lord's Supper is also called the last supper, because it was the last supper Jesus ate with his disciples.

Before Jesus was crucified he had one last gathering with his disciples, it was during the time of the Passover. As they were eating Jesus mentioned that one of his disciples would betray him, everyone was questioning Jesus was it them but Jesus said *"He who dipped his hand with Me in the dish will betray Me."* (Matthew 26:23) NKJV

Jesus took bread, blessed, broke it and gave it to his disciples saying;

Luke 22:19

> *"This is My body which is given for you; do this in remembrance of me."* NKJV

Then Jesus took the cup and gave thanks and offered it to the disciples saying;

Matthew 26:27-29

> *"Drink from it all of you,*
>
> *For this is My blood of the new covenant, which is shed for many for the remission of sins.*

But I say to you I will not drink of his fruit of the vine from now on until the day when I drink it new with you in My Father's kingdom." NKJV

After Jesus and his disciples sang a hymn they went out to the Mount of Olives. (30)

There is no actual celebration date to perform the Lord's Supper as with other holidays. Some religions perform the Lord's Supper every Saturday or Sunday, others perform the Lord's Supper on a certain day of the month or once a year.

1st Corinthians 11:17-34

Paul continued his letter to the church of Corinth concerning the Lord's Supper when partaking of the elements (bread and wine); he mentioned to them that they were performing the Lords' Supper improperly:

They should not consider the Lord's Supper as a feast but it should be more honorable when the congregation come together to have the Lord's Supper. They must have already eaten at their own homes so when they come together no one is hungry or thirsty. (18-22 and 31-34)

Paul reminded them of the Lord's Supper that took place with Jesus and his disciples. He also stated that whoever takes the bread and wine unworthy shall be guilty of the body and blood of the Lord. (23-27)

Everyone must first examine themselves then let all eat and drink of the bread and wine respectively. For if any one eats and drink of the bread and wine unworthy approach causes damnation to themselves. (28-29)

Again, we need to examine ourselves to see if we are spiritually worthy of taking the Lord's Supper.

The bread and wine is called communion, 1st Corinthians 10:16-17.

Self-reflection: if you have done anything wrong towards someone or vice versa whether in words or actions, go to that person and make it right then partake of the communion.

Because these elements are a representation of Jesus Christ, and should not to be taken likely, our lives depend on doing what is right in the sight of God.

DISCERNMENT

The ability to distinguish between what is righteous and what is wicked.

1st Corinthians 2:12-14

> "Now we have received, not the spirit of the world, but the spirit which is of God; that we might know the things that are freely given to us of God.
>
> Which things also we speak, not in the words which man's wisdom teacheth, but which the Holy Ghost teacheth; comparing spiritual things with spiritual,
>
> But the natural man receiveth not the things of the Spirit of God, for they are foolishness unto him: neither can he know them, because they are spiritually discerned." KJV

Hebrews 4:12

> "For the word of God is living and powerful, and sharper than any two-edged sword, piercing even to the division of soul and spirit, and of joints and marrow, and is a discerner of the thoughts and intent of the heart." NKJV

Hebrews 5:13-14

As a babe in Christ means you are still learning of God's righteousness and you are not yet able to discern from good and evil, but those that are full of age are on solid food meaning that they have a long, personal spiritual relationship with God, they are able to discern from good and evil.

Discernment is also a spiritual gift, 1st Corinthians 12:10.

SPIRITUAL GIFTS

1st Corinthians Chapter 12, Paul wrote a letter of church Corinth, about the Spiritual gifts given to individuals to edify the glory of God within the ministry and for the congregation collectively.

Though each person will receive different gifts it still comes from the same Spirit. The Spiritual gifts will benefit all in the house of prayer:

12:8-11

> "For to one is given the word of wisdom through the Spirit, to another the word of knowledge through the same Spirit,
>
> To another faith by the same Spirit, to another the gift of healings by the same Spirit,
>
> To another the working of miracles, to another prophecy, to another discerning of spirits, to another different kinds of tongues, to another the interpretation of tongues."
>
> "But one and the same Spirit works all these things, distributing to each other one individually as He wills."
> NKJV

These gifts were not just given in Paul's time, but right now in our time. We can ask God for a spiritual gift and if God sees fit to bless us with the gift, it will not only benefit the ministry of God but all who are baptized believers in the edification of the house of prayer, individually and collectively.

SPEAKING IN TONGUES

This refers back to Spiritual Baptism:

Speaking in tongues is a Spiritual gift from the Holy Spirit.

1ˢᵗ Corinthians 14: 2

> *"For he who speaks in tongue does not speak to men but to God, for no one understands him; however, in the spirit he speaks mysteries."*

> *"He who speaks in a tongue edifies himself…"* (4) NKJV

Acts 1:8-9, Jesus was speaking to his disciples just before ascending to heaven, for when they would receive the Holy Spirit and its power, and how it would allow them to witness to the nations the gospel of Jesus Christ, then he was taken up in a cloud out of the disciple's sight.

Acts 2:1-4

> *"When the Day of Pentecost had fully come, they were all with one accord in one place.*

> *And suddenly there came a sound from heaven as of a rushing mighty wind, and it filled the whole house where they were sitting.*

*Then there appeared to them divided tongues, as of fire,
and one sat upon each of them*

*And they were filled with the Holy Spirit and began
to speak with other tongues, as the Spirit gave them
utterance.*" NKJV

Day of Pentecost is a yearly Christian celebration of the Holy Spirit
falling down on Jesus' disciples and other baptized believers.

PROPHESY

Is another gift from the Holy Spirit, this gift edifies the church:

1st Corinthians 14:1

> "Pursue love and desire spiritual gifts, but especially that you may prophesy,"

> "But he who prophesies speaks edification and exhortation and comfort to men." (3)

> "…but he who prophesies edifies the church." (4)

> I wish you all spoke with tongues, but even more that you prophesied; for he who prophesies is greater than he who speaks with tongues, unless indeed he interprets, that the church may receive edification. (5)

> But now, brethren, if I come to you speaking with tongues, what shall I profit unless I speak to you either by revelation, by knowledge, by prophesying, or by teaching?" (6) NKJV

Paul was informing the church in Corinth, that it was good to speak in tongues but so much better to prophecy because it would benefit them to receive edification, encouragement, and support towards the church (baptized believers).

THE PASSOVER

The Passover is the observance of God passing over the land of Egypt freeing the Children of Israel from Pharaoh:

Exodus 11:

God told Moses that about midnight he was going out as a midst among Egypt, and that the firstborn in the land would die, from Pharaoh's firstborn, the firstborn of the female servants and hand mill, and to the of firstborn of the animals. (4-5)

This plaque that would come upon Egypt was an outcry in the land that was never heard before and will ever be heard again. (6)

But the Children of Israel and their animals were not cursed under this plague. (7)

Exodus 12:

God instructed Moses and Aaron, that every man in the household of the Israelites, kill a lamb and if the household is too small share it with neighbors that nothing should be wasted. The lamb is to be without blemish, one year old male, and could be a sheep or a goat. (3-5)

At twilight all of Israel should prepare the sheep or goat, they should use some of the blood; put it on two doorposts and on the beam above the doorway. (6-7)

God gave direction on how to cook the meat, when to eat it with unleavened bread and with bitter herbs. (8)

The meat had to be roasted not boiled in water or eaten raw, but roasted in fire with it head, tail, entrails. (9)

None of the meat should remain till morning, if so; the meat would be burned with fire. (11)

The Israelites must be fully dressed with sandals on their feet as they are eating and staffs in their hands ready to flee quickly; this is the Lord's Passover. Because he will pass over the land of Egypt and kill the first-borns, against all that is in Egypt, their gods, man and beast, for God is the Lord. (12)

The blood on the doorposts and on the beam above the door is the sign that he would pass over them and the plague would not come upon them as he passed over the land of Egypt. (13)

God instructed to Moses to observe the Feast of the Unleavened Bread, on the first to the seventh day no one is to eat leavened bread it should be removed from the homes, but whoever eats leavened bread is separated from Israel. They should observe throughout their generations forever. (15-17)

This observance will be a reminder of how God freed the Children of Israel and delivered them to the land he had promised. (24-27).

CARNAL

Carnal is pertaining to the flesh, and it opposes the spirit

Romans 7: 13-24

Paul was stating that are two laws or natures that struggle with each other daily, which are, the flesh and the spirit. Though he wanted to do well in the spirit his flesh had other plans for him to do badly.

Then Paul questioned who would deliver him from his body of death, for he felt he was a wretched man, however, Paul went on to say:

> "I thank God through Jesus Christ our Lord. So then with the mind I; myself serve the law of God but with the flesh the law of sin." (25) NKJV

Self-reflection: Though we have the carnal side of us which can lead to sin we also have the Spirit of God in us to deliver us from trying to do evil.

1st Corinthians 3:1

> "And I, brethren could not speak unto you as unto spiritual but as unto carnal even as unto babes in Christ.

I have fed you with milk and not with meat for hitherto ye were not able to bear it, neither yet now are ye able. (2)

For ye are yet carnal for whereas there is among you envying and strife, and divisions, are ye not carnal and walk as men." (3) KJV

Carnal thinking hinders spiritual growth!!!

As I mentioned previously, a baptized believer who is just learning about God in the ministry is considered a babe in Christ on milk, while a baptized believer who has had a longer or seasoned relationship with God is considered to be eating meat.

We do not need to hinder the babes in Christ for their lack of knowledge about the word of God because we were once like them and we do not need to cause anger among those that are seasoned in their knowledge because we are all trying to reach the same goal, to spend eternity in heaven.

We all can learn something from each other, for God wants us to do things decent and in order for his glory.

3 AND 7

These numbers are special in the Bible and are memorable events:

1st John 5:7, 3 are in Heaven; God, Jesus and the Holy Spirit.

Jonah 1:17, Jonah stayed in the belly of a fish for 3 days and 3 nights.

Matthew 27:63, Jesus rose from the dead after lying in a tomb for 3 days.

Acts 9:9, Saul whom became Paul was struck with blindness for three day before receiving his sight.

Genesis 2: 1-3, God created the world in 6 days, on the 7th day God rested and called it the Sabbath. Mentioned previously in this book, that man was to observe this day as the Lord's Day.

THE TITLE

God's Bibliography: in his own words, it is a lot to take in with this title, I know right? I was at a loss for words when it was given to me to write, I thought it would be wrong but it is not, when people write their biographies what they mention are the important aspects in their lives, such as journeys, adventures, and other important things they have accomplished.

This is actually what this book is about, some important facts about God from spiritual men whom were inspired by him, through the Holy Spirit, to write the Holy Bible. They were able to record his greatness, power and majesty; these scriptures are by no means mythical or fantasies coming from someone's imaginations but true words from God.

Please don't be confused when it comes to God's word because they are true and don't be left in the dark (spiritually blind) to the ways of God, how you decide will determine heaven or hell for you, your choice, **OWN IT!!!**

Again, these are just some of the golden nuggets that can be found in the Holy Bible, my desire for you; is that this will inspire you to read the word of God and apply it to your daily life.

I also hope this book will instill longing for God and that it will moves hearts, mind, souls and spirits to come to him before it is too late. I pray for all to seek God, learn of his Love as He Loves us! God Bless you all!

Romans 8:39

> "Neither height nor depth, nor anything else in all creation, will be able to separate us from the LOVE of GOD that is in CHRIST JESUS OUR LORD!!!" NIV

1st John 4:8

> "He who does not love does not know God for GOD IS LOVE." NKJV

ABOUT THE AUTHOR

The book is based on the Holy Bible and topic that God has inspired me to provide to this world today, because now is the time for Truth and to set apart from this world that has become distant from God. This book will enable the reader to start a relationship or build a better one with God for he longs for his children before its to late.

Carol Kilpatrick, mother of three, love the word of God and was inspired to write this book.

Printed in the United States
by Baker & Taylor Publisher Services